Prairie Five-0

Dave Peskor

Prairie Five-0
Copyright © 2020 by Dave Peskor

Tellwell Talent
www.tellwell.ca

ISBN
978-0-2288-2548-7 (Hardcover)
978-0-2288-2546-3 (Paperback)
978-0-2288-2547-0 (eBook)

Preface

I had a career in law enforcement that spanned more than forty years. From my first days as a boy soldier in the Canadian Military Police Reserve, followed by several years as an Alberta Provincial Correctional Officer; to small town policing in Redcliff, Alberta and finally, the completion of my calling with the Medicine Hat Police Service.

This is not a "blood-stained badge" cop novel. I am not going to recount the horror, gore and inhumanity we all witnessed as police officers. This book is not about the action that makes TV cop shows and movies popular, nor is it about finding a colleague alone and crying in the locker room. Those are different stories.

This book is about the funny and sometimes amazingly absurd events we encountered as we strove to Serve and Protect. Policing changed me as a person and largely defined who I am. During my career, I embraced the humour I found, no matter how dark that comedy may have been. As police officers, sometimes we'd call it tombstone humour. It helped to remind us that we are still human.

The stories in this book are all true and verifiable. By that I mean that the events happened to me personally, or I witnessed those events, or I was told of what happened by a trusted and reliable source. With respect to the latter, well you can't make this stuff up and if it ain't true, it should be.

I make no apology for the language used in my stories. That was the dialect of the day and the scenes would not be properly set if I wrote otherwise.

The characters in this book are all real people. I have purposely written some of the stories without using full names or I have changed the names slightly. In several stories, persons are identified by their real full name, but I have done so with their knowledge, or in the case of those now deceased, with fond memories and respect.

This project has been a trip down Memory Lane. I found that the more I remembered, the more I remembered. I would like to acknowledge those people who were instrumental in the writing of this book. First and foremost, thanks to my wife Margot, who encouraged me to pursue my dream and who endured my many requests for her to read this passage or that. Also, I wish to acknowledge my former colleagues who contributed by confirming my recollection of once long forgotten tales. And finally, for the overwhelming support and encouragement I received from family, friends and those former colleagues who "beta-tested" my stories over social media, Cheers to you all!

Dave Pedor
Redcliff, Alberta

Prologue

And so, it began.

It was my first day in a police uniform. I checked my look in the mirror. No time yet to have the shirt and pants tailored to properly fit my slim build, but they were clean and pressed with creases like razor blades. Hat on straight, but with an ever so slight angle for attitude, and leather Sam Browne duty belt polished to a shiny black. I was not quite twenty-three years old. I weighed in at one hundred and forty-seven and one-half pounds with a well trimmed moustache, the type we all grew at that age, believing it made us look older and more mature. When people later asked me why so many young cops sported moustaches, I used to say that they were issued in Cop School. I said that I had asked for a "pencil thin Latino-style moustache", but the Quartermaster said only the girls were allowed to wear those.

Then I stood in front of the mirror and did what so many had done before me. I drew my gun and checked out my reflection to see if I had the determined gaze that would make a criminal's blood run cold. I suppose there are those who will deny ever doing that when they first started their career. I think their credibility may be suspect. So, now I stand in front of the mirror to reflect on my career, and I have concluded it was a damn good ride.

Table of Contents

1. Small Town

2. Do You D.U.I.?

3. All for Fun

4. Military Police

5. British Army

9. Big City Cops

10. City Cells

16. Cigarettes

Small Town

Yikes!

I discovered that you know you're in trouble when, during a high-speed pursuit and usually in the middle of a curve, you drop the radio microphone through the spokes of the steering wheel.

Shhhhh!

One summer afternoon I was driving slowly in my Patrol car along a street bordered on one side by residential homes and on the other side by an undeveloped field of prairie grass. The field teemed with wildlife at that time and it was not unusual to spot a jackrabbit or even a coyote. At dusk and dawn, Mule Deer and Pronghorn Antelope also frequented the area. But the plain old Gopher was the most common species found there.

I saw a group of three young boys, all about five or six years old, sitting about twenty yards from the road. They were staring intently at something. My curiosity got the best of me so I stopped and walked up to them. As I approached, three little hands with index fingers extended went to their lips in a gesture that silently said, "Shhhhh". I crept closer to the boys and whispered, "What are you doing?" The boldest of the three pointed to a cardboard box propped up on an angle by a stick. The stick had a piece of string tied to it; the other end being held by one of the lads who stared intently at the Gopher hole it balanced over. "We're trapping Beavers!"

I Could've Been a Cowboy

On a sunny summer day just after I started with the Redcliff Town Police Department, I received a dispatch about cattle being loose on a secondary access road near the Trans Canada Highway. I arrived on scene minutes later and sure enough, there were about thirty cows munching on grass in the ditch and lazily standing on the asphalt, having escaped through a hole in the fence a short distance away.

Now I'm a city boy, born and raised. To this day, the only horse I've ever ridden was when I was about six years old, inside the Safeway grocery store. My Mom put a dime in the machine and I merrily galloped away for about two minutes on my trusty ceramic steed. What the heck was I going to do about these cows? And I had a group of stalled motorists waiting to see what the heck I was going to do as well.

I hoped that the principles of crowd control might just overlap the boundary of species and turned on my overhead emergency lights. Afterall, I had to do something. So, I got on the P.A. system and announced in my most official voice, "Okay you cows, THIS-IS-THE-POLICE! Move in an orderly fashion towards the hole in the fence!"

Darned if they didn't start to move. I followed along slowly, urging them on. Motorists were laughing and urging me on. I soon had the unruly herd through the fence and safely back in their pasture.

Applause and honks from the crowd I had entertained. Now I know that it was just the flashing lightbar and noise from the P.A. system speaker that got them "doggies" moving, but what the heck, I'm a Cowboy!

Our Cops

I was a young police officer employed by the Town of Redcliff Police Department. Back in those days the population of Redcliff was barely three thousand people.

In the summertime a mix of small-town kids and rural kids often held "bush parties" down the steep hill road to the local river bottom. One or two policemen cannot effectively disperse one or two hundred barely-of-age teens, especially when "wobbly pops" are involved.

So, we would make our presence known, instruct them to keep the bonfire under control, clean up their mess before they left and warn them that there would be "all Hell to pay" if we found any youngsters there. For the most part, they respected us and complied with that instruction.

Occasionally we took a little "sass", but not usually from the locals. I remember having given the standard "bush party" caution when several young men from the neighboring City of Medicine Hat started to get in my face. That ended very quickly when two Redcliff brothers, both big and beefy, gave them an ominous warning. "These are OUR cops. We can fuck with them... you can't!"

Faceoff

Late one summer weekend night I received a call from the R.C.M.P. Telecoms Centre in Red Deer, Alberta. Two of their Medicine Hat members were outnumbered at a "bush party" at the Redcliff river bottom and were calling for back up. I was the only Redcliff Town Police member on duty, but when a fellow cop calls for help, you go!

As I approached the area, I saw a large bonfire. On one side stood the two R.C.M.P. members and on the other side, a large group of local teens. I parked my car and walked down the middle towards the standoff. It must have surprised the Mounties when I didn't go to their side. Instead, I waded into the crowd of Redcliff teens. I knew most of them and they all knew me. A few moments later, I waved the Mounties to my side. Some big boys patted them on the back and apologized for causing any concern. A few of the girls gave them hugs and told them how handsome they were in their uniforms.

The R.C.M.P. members were astounded. Hopefully, that lesson in "Police Community Relations" served them well in later postings.

Sage Advice

I was driving my patrol car on Broadway Avenue, the main street through Redcliff, Alberta. It was a beautiful summer evening and I found myself following behind a copper-coloured 1969 Dodge Dart. The driver slowed in the westbound lane and signalled to turn left, across the single solid line. The turn was completed and the driver angle parked in front of a local convenience store. I activated my overhead emergency lights and pulled along side. As I approached the car, I saw a very nice-looking woman who was well known to me.

I said, "Ma'am, the Alberta Highway Traffic Act prohibits the crossing of a single solid line unless you are accessing off-street parking. You have not parked "off street". She looked at me in disbelief and said, "Seriously? You're going to give me a ticket?"

I remembered some sage advice I was once given. "Happy wife...happy life". So, I said with a grin, "No Hon, I'll let you off with a warning...this time."

Santa's Helpers

Travel on that particular Christmas Eve was not looking too promising. Early in the day the sky started getting greyer and greyer and the temperature plummeted. Soon the winds whipped up and we were in the midst of a full-blown Prairie blizzard.

A yellow Alberta Department of Highways truck pulled up in front of the old Redcliff Police Station and the driver walked in. He was a pleasant gentleman, soon to be retired by the look of his weathered, wrinkled skin and white beard. He advised us that the highways were ordered closed and asked, would we please man the barricades?

We helped the older man set up his barricades and flashing lights on the far side of town and began to stop all traffic headed west toward Calgary. No sooner had we done this when the storm became an entire "white out" with visibility down to twenty or thirty feet on the unsheltered highway.

Most people were very understanding, and some were sympathetic, as they sat in their warm cars or went to local restaurants to wait out the storm while we stood outside freezing. The professional drivers in their big rigs just shrugged their shoulders and said, "Okay". One told us he was going to put some "sleep time" into his logbook and could we please wake him when the roads were clear. A local banker was very understanding and opened his vault after-hours for the armoured car that was stranded here.

One man was determined to get to Calgary in time for the family Christmas get together, even if he killed his own family in the process. When I denied him passage, he said to me, "You're just trying to spoil OUR Christmas because YOU have to work!".

Now it was Christmas, so I decided to be polite and just walk away, although his lack of understanding left this young Policeman shaking his head.

Later that afternoon, Santa arrived in a bright yellow Department of Highways truck. It was the old man that had notified us of the road closure. He got out of his truck holding a large brown paper sack. "You boys go sit in your cars and warm up, I'll hold down the fort for awhile". Inside the bag we found steaming hot cups of coffee and grilled cheese sandwiches.

An hour or so after, we were able to open the highway to traffic and as people drove by, everyone honked their horn or wished us a Merry Christmas...well, almost everyone.

Uplifting

After all these years, many thanks to that lady who lived in Redcliff. The one who, when she saw a Police car coming down the street, smiled and stood in her front picture window as she lifted her shirt. That display of support really boosted the morale of our nightshift crew.

The Gooberment

In the Province of Alberta, civilian oversight of policing is provided by Commissions or Committees. These bodies do not direct police operations, but contribute by helping to establish policies, participate in planning and allocate necessary funding. The Commissions normally are a mix of appointed volunteer citizens from within the community with representation by elected members of the local municipal Council.

In the mid-eighties, the population of the Town of Redcliff was just over 3800. As a result, the elected Town Council did not consist of, nor was its various boards filled with, Doctors, Lawyers, Scientists or Business Professionals.

One of the elected Town Council members who sat on the Redcliff Police Commission was a local small businessman. He and his family had come to Canada in the early 1950's and he spoke with an accent that identified him as being a first-generation European immigrant. He also made no effort to conceal his disdain for the police. Despite our Member's post-secondary education, training and experience, he publicly regarded us as nothing better than common labourers.

The Chief of Police had an out of town commitment and so, as Sergeant, I was instructed to attend the next scheduled Police Commission meeting in his place. One of the Agenda items was news of a Provincial Government proposal to implement an Alberta-wide Police radio network. Even though the proposal would come at minimal or no cost to the Town, the Council member was opposed in principle and couldn't understand the need for such a thing. He said it would be, in his mind, wasteful spending by the "Gooberment".

I tried to explain that it would facilitate inter-agency communications during disasters or even events as common as police pursuits through multiple jurisdictions. He asked, "Why don't they just send up the Provincial helicopter?"

I asked, "The Provincial helicopter? What helicopter?" He said, "The Provincial helicopter! You know! The Airwolf!"

I was stunned. The room went silent for a moment before the Chairman of the Police Commission assured the Councilor that "the Airwolf" was just a fictional craft in a made-for-TV action series. The Councilor shook his head and I'm not sure he was convinced that we had no access to such resources.

Who? Me?

Constable Bill Dagg came to us from the Calgary Police Department. He was always a "big city" Copper at heart. As such, he sometimes had a "failure to communicate" with small town citizens. One day, as he drove his marked patrol car past the Town of Redcliff Post Office, he spotted a local suspect he needed to talk to about a recent offence.

The Redcliff Post Office was the "heart" of the town. People went there everyday to collect their mail, visit with other town folk, and maybe band together for a coffee at the local bakery.

Bill rolled down his driver's side window. Leaning his head out, he called to the suspect in his loudest, most authorative voice, "HEY STUPID!!" Everyone on the street stopped dead in their tracks and looked towards the Police car.

Bill casually looked at the nearest civilian, then pointed to the bad guy as he said, "Not you STUPID, him STUPID!"

Oh Deer

This would never stand the test of fairness today, but years ago we were allowed to catch bad guys without worry about whether or not we "played fair" ...as long as it was legal...somehow.

I had confidential source information that a certain man had in his possession, a stolen snowmobile engine. I didn't have sufficient grounds for a search warrant, but the man did have a garage door with a window that faced directly onto his back alley. Curiosity got the better of me and late one night, I confess, I did take a peek through that window.

I saw a deer carcass hanging in the garage. Now this wasn't even close to hunting season, so I presumed that the deer had been poached illegally. Did I see a stolen snowmobile engine? No, but I did see a large shape covered by a tarp that could have been a snowmobile engine...or perhaps another poached deer.

I still felt that I had no grounds for a search warrant but advised the local Fish & Wildlife officer of the suspected poached deer. In those days, the Frog, Log and Bog officers had more far-reaching powers of search and seizure than ordinary municipal police officers. They didn't, at that time, need much more than suspicion to legally enter the garage.

Of course, being by himself, and for officer safety purposes, he officially requested assistance from the local Police while he conducted his investigation. We made the entry and did indeed find a poached deer carcass inside the garage. That tarp did not cover another poached deer. It concealed a snowmobile engine that had recently been reported as stolen.

The Night Watchman

It just takes some guys a little while longer to realize their calling. This Constable was once a Policeman. Now he is a Fireman.

He was on patrol early one summer morning and stopped to "shake hands" with the back door of a closed highway gas station restaurant. Imagine his surprise when the door opened.

The Constable crept inside and lo and behold, he found a man sleeping inside the restaurant kitchen. The man woke with a start and then, seeing it was a Policeman, he relaxed. "Oh, thank God it's you.... I'm the new night watchman...I must have fell asleep...if you'd been the boss, I'd be fired!"

The night watchman begged the Constable not to tell his boss that he had been found sleeping and even offered to brew a pot of fresh coffee for them to share. The offer was graciously declined and the Constable assured the man he wouldn't tell his boss. He cautioned him about sleeping on the job and with that, left the premises.

So, about an hour later a call came in from the gas station. It was from the owner. There had been a break in. "No Constable, we don't have a night watchman...why do you ask?"

Happy Birds Day

I was a young Constable recently employed by the Town of Redcliff Police Department. We had a very small Police Force at that time; a Chief, a Sergeant, and four Constables. Our civilian staff was one young gal who served as steno and dispatcher. Obviously, she couldn't work 24-7.

After normal business hours and on weekends, our incoming calls for service were routed through what was at that time, a marvel of technology. The telephone company installed a device that would automatically transfer incoming telephone calls to our radios. You phoned the Police...we heard a beep on our radio and, after pushing a button...magic! We had your telephone call on the air. The town gossips with police scanner radios loved it!

It was my birthday and I was working alone on a weekend day shift. At about 1:00 p.m. I stopped at a highway gas station restaurant for lunch. I had just started eating my sandwich when a call came in on my portable radio.

I answered, "Redcliff Police". The response was a tiny little voice, that sang to me with a heavy German-Canadian accent, "Happy Birds-Day to You, Happy Birds-Day to You". It was my Mother-in-law, calling from Calgary. I let her finish her Birthday greeting and thanked her for calling. After she hung up, I looked around and saw that the whole Restaurant had heard our conversation.

I turned a little red-in-the-face when one of the waitresses appeared with a cupcake. It had a single burning birthday candle, and the whole restaurant, staff and customers, sang to me, "Happy Birds-Day".

I Spy with My Little Eye

The caller was irate and obviously very much offended. His neighbors, a young married couple residing directly across the street from him, had the nerve to engage in sexual relations in their living room, with drapes wide open on the picture window for all to see. It must have been quite the picture. Believe me, we arrived as quickly as we could, but the act was over. I saw nothing.

Our complainant explained that he had peered across the street and saw the naked couple locked in the embraces of passion. Standing on his front step, I looked across the street at the neighbor's window. "Sir, that window is probably fifty yards from here...how could you possibly see what was going on in there?"

Indignantly, he produced a set of binoculars and said, "Well, we have to go upstairs to my bedroom. You get a better angle from there".

Granny's Crowbar

I was a young Policeman weighing in at the not so substantial one hundred forty-seven and one-half pounds. A good portion of that weight was the moustache I had grown to make myself "look older".

One afternoon, a breathless woman rushed into the Town of Redcliff Police station screaming that her husband had gone psychotic and was chasing her, intent on taking her life. Just then, a telephone call came in reporting that the aforementioned gentleman was presently crashing through the fence of an elderly lady neighbor of the Police station. I ran out the back door and almost into the arms of my suspect.

The fight was on. As we rolled around on the ground, I felt his teeth cutting into my finger. He outweighed me and I couldn't restrain this madman, so I just kept pummeling him for all I was worth.

After what seemed like an eternity my youthful stamina, and a generous serving of knuckle sandwich, began to give me a gain on this wildman. Just then one of our office cleaning staff ambled up. He said to me half-heartedly, "Do you need some help?" Breathlessly I choked out, "Just sit on him!" With the added weight pinning the man down I was able to apply the handcuffs and take him into custody.

When I returned from booking my prisoner into cells our Secretary, Vonda Brost, was laughing about my "back up". I thought she was referring to the cleaner, but she soon corrected me.

It seems that while I was fighting tooth and nail with my suspect the elderly neighbor lady whose fence was damaged saw the fracas. According to Vonda, this little old lady grabbed a crowbar and said to the nearby men watching the fight, "If no one's going to help that Policeman, I AM!"

Shlake and Blake

Irwin was one of our best friends. We watched as Irwin and his family built the Happiness Gardens Chinese Restaurant in Redcliff, Alberta from the ground up, block-by-block. He, along with his wife Minnie and his brother Norman, were also involved in the venture.

Irwin's family restaurant made the finest Chinese food in the area, attracting customers from as far away as Saskatchewan, who made the trip for one of their meals following an afternoon of tax-reduced shopping in nearby Medicine Hat.

Irwin and Norman became very close to the local Police. We took the brothers to hunt and fish with us. Our children went to school together.

One night my partner, Bill Sharpe, and I stopped into the restaurant for coffee. Irwin asked us if we had ever eaten squid. Neither of us had and eagerly accepted his offer of a taste. A huge plate of rice covered with succulent squid dressed with their special black bean sauce was instantly presented.

Irwin informed us that this was a treat. It was not on the menu, but a dish served only to the family members who worked in the restaurant. It was delicious.

Several months later, Bill and I were again having coffee with Irwin. Bill hinted that he was a little hungry. He asked Irwin, "What did you cook up for the family supper tonight?" Irwin said, "Pork Chops". Bill asked hopefully, "Did you cook them Western style or Chinese style?" When Irwin replied, "Western style" I said, "What's that? Shlake and Blake?"

Irwin paused a moment, thinking about what I had said, and then muttered with a wide grin, "Fluck You".

Wrong Ingredient

Irwin's mom and dad were a cute older couple. I smiled as he brought them before me at the police station. They spoke limited English and looked so apprehensive. I only needed to sign off on their passport applications and when I did, I saw a wave of relief on their faces. That gave me a different perspective about how police are viewed by other cultures.

So, it was almost hunting season. I was having a sandwich at the lunch counter in the Happiness Gardens Restaurant and glanced towards the kitchen entrance. Irwin's Dad must have been standing on his tippy-toes so he could see out the kitchen doors in-out windows. He waved and then came out and spoke to me. He knew we were going deer hunting soon. His request was simple, "bring me deer tail".

I said "Okay," but asked why he wanted deer tails. Irwin's Dad looked around to see if anyone could overhear and then whispered, "I make soup". He saw that I was puzzled and then said with a smirk, "Make your pecker hard!"

Well, I cut off and collected the tail from every deer I and my buddies harvested and gave them all to Irwin's Dad.

A few weeks later I asked him how it worked out. Sadly, he shook his head and said, "Must have been wrong kind of deer".

Would You Like a Bigger Shovel?

Wildlife tends to retreat upon man's encroachment into its territory. That's why we don't have many snake complaints anymore. Back in the 70's, the Town of Redcliff was not nearly as developed as it is now and during the summer months, we were regularly called upon to capture and remove rattlesnakes from residential yards.

My first encounter with a real, live Rattlesnake left me petrified. I had been summoned to a residence where the caller had found the critter holed up in her yard....and she expected me to do something about it. My suggestion of live and let live fell on deaf ears.

In the years to come we would receive some training from the Provincial Wildlife officers in how to deal with snakes and we obtained the proper equipment to aid in their capture. But for now, all I had was a shovel and one very pissed off snake.

I decided that it was in the best interests of Humankind to eliminate the critter. I reared back and swung my short shovel, neatly clipping the snake across the head. The snake reared back in response and hissed. The lady homeowner broke the standoff by saying to me, "Would you like a bigger shovel?"

That's when the snake and I called a truce. I decided not to go any nearer to him, and he decided to slither away from the yard.

Doc Says You're Gonna' Die

Well we did eventually get some training in the capture of Rattlesnakes. At one time, the Province of Alberta designated the Rattlesnake to be a "Protected Species" so that meant no more whacking them with a too short shovel. It was catch and release.

We were issued with a sturdy, aluminum "snake catching pole". Provincial Wildlife officers taught us to tighten the metal cable loop at the end of the pole around the fattest part of the snake, not the head or neck, so as not to damage these delicate little flowers of the Prairie. Okay...sure.

My partner, Brian Roberts, and I were dispatched to a home under construction. The caller pointed to several sheets of plywood leaning up against an outside wall. Sure enough, there was a five-foot long Rattlesnake hiding behind there. No problem, we're trained professionals.

I got the snake pole and Brian held up the heavy burlap bag we used to confine the captured Rattlers prior to their safe release. By now I had enough experience with snakes that I wasn't quite as fearful of them. I deftly looped the cable around the fattest part of the belly, just as we had been instructed. I may have tightened the loop a bit too much but I wasn't taking any chances with this big boy.

Brian stood nearby with the burlap bag open and ready. I was about to place the snake into the bag when all three of us, Brian, and me and the snake, came to the same conclusion. A five-foot long snake, looped in the middle, means that there are two-and-one-half feet of snake hanging down each side.

I started to pull back at the same instant that Brian tried to make his arms longer. The snake lunged out like a shot, its fangs exposed and aimed directly at my partner's crotch. Fortunately, the strike came up short. I quickly broke all the rules and readjusted the loop, tightly around its slim neck. After our Rattler was safely contained in the bag, I thought of an old joke about two cowboys, one of whom who had been bitten in the crotch by a snake, and couldn't help but laugh as I said out loud, "Doc says you're gonna' die".

Bull

My predecessor, Elroy Lafond, was the former Redcliff Police Department Sergeant before he left to join the Medicine Hat Fire Department. He responded to an unremarkable complaint of long forgotten import. It had been very hot that day and as he arrived at the complaint, he foolishly left his car windows down. While he was distracted by the aforementioned call, someone decided to give Elroy a present. Whatever the complaint was, he presumably settled the matter to the satisfaction of everyone involved.

Sergeant Lafond drove off and was several blocks away when he felt something on his leg. Looking down, now no doubt now in sheer terror, he saw a large snake crawling up his leg. Remember that the car was, at this time, still in motion. How he avoided a serious crash and extracted himself from the car is still a mystery.

Now our flavor of Rattlesnake in southern Alberta, and what is commonly called a Bull Snake, are very similar in appearance. The two main differences are that the Bull Snake doesn't have rattles and it is non-venomous. But they can still give you a nasty bite. Somehow Elroy managed to get himself and the snake out of the car in one piece. The snake was then secured and relocated to the open prairie.

Ever the optimist, Elroy proclaimed that he was lucky it had been a Bull Snake in his car that day.

A Buck Three-Ninety

One of my first partners was a Constable named John Unreiner.

John or "Chonny", as he was often called, was raised in Alberta's farming community amongst folks from the towns of Hilda and Schuler and other such rural Alberta places. The languages spoken by the area's settlers and their descendants were a mixture of English, German and Russian. They also created their own unique dialect that they passed on to their children and grandchildren.

It was my first week on the job. John and I had stopped someone for a traffic violation. We had the driver in the back seat of our Police car. John finished serving the traffic ticket to the driver and turned to me. He said, "Leave him out".

I hadn't heard what John had said. He repeated, "Leave him out". I sat there looking blankly at John. "What did you say?" John looked at me like I was a moron, and he once again sternly said, "LEAVE HIM OUT".

"Leave him out?" I thought John was going to explode. Then I got it. Our Police cars were modified so that the door handles did not work from the inside of the rear passenger compartment. John wanted me to let the person out of the back seat. I said, "Oh. You want me to LET HIM OUT of the back?' John started to turn beet red in the face. I quickly jumped out and opened the rear passenger door to "leave" our subject out.

My next lessons involved terms such as "a buck three-ninety" and "side by each".

I'm Not Looking!

People react differently when they are arrested.

If they object, men tend to "cuss out" the police. If they're feeling "tall and strong" they may even fight back. Women may also cuss and sometimes they too, try to fight back. But sometimes women employ a different tactic. They take off their clothes. I think they do this to shock the male officer, and perhaps intimidate him into fearing that he may be deemed to have said or done something inappropriate.

It was my day off, a sunny, summer Sunday morning. Our home telephone rang at about 6:00 A.M. The on-duty Town of Redcliff Police Department Constable was in a panic. Alone and fairly new to the job, he had never experienced such a situation.

He had arrested a woman and she was currently in our holding cell. Every time he checked on her, she bared her chest. "Sarge, I need you to help me with this". So, I dressed and drove to the Police station. The Constable briefed me and I said, "Okay, let's go deal with this".

As he opened the door to the holding cell area, the woman stood up from the bunk and seeing two of us, she took her top completely off. The young Constable recoiled, covered his eyes and as he turned away, he said "I'm not looking". The woman sneered and gave her boobs a jiggle. I took a look...a good long look, and then focused on her eyes. "Put your shirt on woman!", I commanded. She stared for a moment and then complied.

She said to me, "I'll talk to you, but not to him!"

My Good Luck

Gilles Duhaime was a large and sometimes intimidating man, with a bushy beard and a barrel chest. Born in Quebec, he somehow found his way to the Medicine Hat area where he raised his family and ran a successful auto repair business. He put his kids though school and his son still operates the family business to this day. He worked hard as a mechanic by day and, for a period of time, provided contracted towing services for the Redcliff Town Police Department.

One night, I found myself behind his tow truck as it entered Redcliff from the highway to Medicine Hat. My partner for the night was Miles Johnson. Miles and I recognized the tow truck as belonging to Gilles and we both almost simultaneously commented on something out of place. This was a work truck and rarely, if ever, saw a car wash. Bolted to the back of the otherwise grimy truck was a clean, bright and shiny licence plate.

Miles said, "Looks like Gilles got a new plate". He called in for Registry information and we soon learned that:

(a) the plate was currently valid

(b) the plate was not registered to Gilles, and

(c) the plate was not associated to the vehicle it was attached to

So, we pulled him over.

When asked about the licence plate, Gilles grinned and said, with a Francophone accent, "My plate was almost done and I took some garbage to the dump. I looked down and I could not believe my good luck! Who throws away a perfectly good plate with so much time left on it?"

A quick roadside lesson on how vehicle registration works and we then instructed Gilles to "tow his tow truck" to his house where it was to remain until it was properly registered.

Street Cred

Vonda Brost was a young woman, perhaps 18 or 19 years old at the time. It was her first real job off the farm, and her first live-on-your-own apartment, a suite in a local 4-plex. She had accepted a job offer as steno-dispatcher for the Redcliff Town Police Department.

That particular dayshift was extremely hot, and our girl was faced with a long walk because her car was in the shop for repairs. I offered her a ride home.

As we pulled up in front of her address, I saw three young men from a neighboring suite sitting outside, shirtless in the sunshine. Vonda thanked me for the ride and began to stroll across the street to her apartment. I rolled down my window and yelled, "Do not ever, ever, do that again young woman!"

Oh...the walk of shame...but she definitely got some street cred!

You Need A Bigger Towel

By all accounts Eddie never really was quite "normal". When he was very young, his older brother convinced Eddie that if he tied a towel around his neck as a cape, he could fly like Superman. Eddie decided to give it a go. Suitably attired, he climbed to the roof of the family garage and leapt forward, onward...downward. Little Eddie was lying on the ground crying. His big brother walked up and told him where he had gone wrong. "You need a bigger towel".

Eddie had a few other scrapes along the way including a serious car accident that left him with a metal plate in his head. Unfortunately, it also left him a few more steps out of pace.

Somewhere along the line, Stan, a Redcliff Town Police Constable, had done Eddie wrong. Eddie needed to extract his revenge so he climbed onto the roof of the Police Station and waited. Soon a patrol car arrived and the targeted Constable exited. Stan was approaching the front door when he heard something overhead. Looking up, to his surprise, he saw Eddie leaping menacingly from the rooftop, arms outstretched with hands formed like claws.

"To the rear...March!" Stanley took one step backward and watched as Eddie slammed into the cold, hard pavement. You need a bigger towel, Eddie!

Knock, Knock

There were drug traffickers inside the house and we were outside. We came armed with a search warrant crafted by Constable Gerald Boucher and a sledgehammer wielded by Constable Miles Johnson. As Sergeant, I had the Warrant and was accompanied by Gerald and Miles, who was itching to use that hammer. Other members covered the back. I knocked loudly on the front door and announced, "Police! Search Warrant! Open Up!"

Now I honestly thought I heard a scurrying sound from behind the door. I told Miles to "Hit It!" He wielded the ten-pound sledge like a railway man. He hit the flimsy door once, twice, three times and still it failed to give.

Frustrated, he kept pounding blows against the door and still it held solid, despite the frame being reduced nearly to toothpicks. Finally, we heard the bolt unlatch. As the door opened, we saw

Constable Bill Sharpe standing there. He discovered that the back door had been left unlocked.

Our resolve renewed, we all rushed into the premises. We found the occupants upstairs, in a bedroom, fast asleep despite the noise we had made. And yes, we did indeed find drugs inside the house.

Scrub-a-Dub-Dub

The fellow was a grown, almost middle-aged man, who was still living at home with his retired parents in the small town of Redcliff, Alberta, a "bedroom" community of the nearby City of Medicine Hat. He supported himself by rototilling gardens in the Spring and any other odd jobs he could pick up during the rest of the year.

Although he didn't have, nor did he ever have, the body of a Greek God, he fancied himself to be a nude male model. He even offered his services to the local College Arts faculty but was rebuffed. Undaunted, he turned to photography and produced a number of self-portraits, including his most famous, "nude on a child's rocking horse wearing nothing but a cowboy hat and boots". He also "creeped on" under-age teenage girls at the local video arcade until the owner asked us to put the run on him.

One evening, he made a complaint of fraud to the police. It seemed that, seeking some relief, he decided to engage the services of a local prostitute. She accompanied him to a rather seedy Medicine Hat hotel where the act was to take place.

Now renting a hooker is similar to renting this type of hotel room. When you rent the room, you pay before you stay. When renting a hooker, you pay before you play. The price was agreed upon and money exchanged hands. The lady could not help but notice that her customer was really, really not up on his personal hygiene. She offered to run a nice, warm bath and scrub him up before they had their fun. He enthusiastically accepted.

She did give him a good scrubbing with a stiff brush, presumably one that she found near the toilet. Scrubbed red, she told him to towel off while she got ready. When he emerged from the bathroom, the hooker, and his cash, were gone. She made a clean getaway.

I Didn't See That Coming

She was a young woman, maybe twenty-one or twenty-two years old. She was from out of town, only here in Redcliff for a week of stripping at a local club. She called me to her hotel room because she was fearful. By mid-week there was a customer who showed "too much" interest in her. She was afraid. As we talked, she gave me as much information as she could about the creep. I tried to reassure her that we would do whatever we could to protect her.

I continued my investigation when she said, "I have to get dressed for my next set, do you mind?" I said, "Of course not" but expected that she would change in the bathroom and we would carry on our conversation through the door from there.

Nope. She dropped her robe and my jaw dropped as she stood there, totally naked, and I witnessed my first ever, "reverse striptease".

The Stakeout

It was my first real "stakeout."

Our complainant was the owner of a vacant home undergoing renovation. During the course of the previous several weeks someone had been breaking into the premises during the dark hours, making a mess, causing damage, and stealing tools.

The owner of the property cooperated fully. He knew our plans and showed me around the place. He pointed to a back door that appeared to be especially flimsy. "They sometimes come in through there," said the property owner. I told him that if we saw anyone in the premises, that would be our way in.

Our stakeout was long and boring. My partner for that night decided that he would look less like a cop if he wore a long, brown wig to cover his short hair. I guess we needed all the help we could get...two young guys sitting in a copper-coloured 1969 Dodge Dart, lights out and engine running, a half block from our target. Our boredom was broken by a telephone complaint over our mobile phone from a gravelly-voiced citizen who we all knew well.

"Town Police."

"Yeah, there's two guys in a brown car been sitting here all night."

"Okay, who's calling?"

"I want to remain anonymous."

"Okay John, thanks for calling, we'll check it out."

Just then, we both saw movement from inside the building. My partner and I excitedly ran from our car to the back door. I had prepared for this moment for a long time. Flashlight in one hand, and revolver in the other, I reared back and yelled "Police, don't move". I then gave the flimsy back door a vicious kick. The door held solid. I felt pain shoot up the length of my right leg. Confused, I booted the door again, and again. Still it didn't budge. We then resorted to breaking out a small window and unceremoniously climbing in. Surprisingly, we still found our suspect cowering in a corner.

After we secured our prisoner and once again felt heroic, I checked out the back door. The owner later told us that he had thought about our plan and felt it would be more realistic if the door was secured. He nailed it shut with several six-inch spikes.

Just a Burp

I was about twenty-two years old when I was ordered to attend my first autopsy. Ken Ingram was the senior Member assigned to accompany me, and he assured me that everything would be okay. He then went on to gleefully describe, in gory detail, some of the previous autopsies he had witnessed.

I was intrigued at the thought of seeing a human being laid open with all the internal mystery and machinery in plain view. But I was scared and didn't want to pass out or lose my breakfast. I knew I would never live down such a reaction. The autopsy was scheduled for first thing the next morning.

I have always started my day with a cup of good coffee. That morning I had two or three cups to steady my nerves. I had also foregone breakfast, just in case. We arrived on time and the autopsy started. Everything went "by the book" and I was captivated by the procedure. In the years that followed I witnessed dozens of autopsies and each one was fascinating. When I was in the room with a Pathologist who was passionate about his science, I found that I absorbed knowledge like a sponge. I also found those same passionate Pathologists willing and eager to spend some extra time with an ordinary Policeman who was truly showing some interest. I've even had a Medical Examiner who wouldn't let me leave before he showed me several other M.E. cases that were interesting, even though they were no part of my investigation.

Ken stood a step ahead of me and to my left. When the Pathologist commented that he had found something interesting, I leaned forward over Ken's right shoulder to get a better look.

That's when I burped. It was just the three cups of coffee and no breakfast. It was just a simple burp. Ken recoiled back like a bolt of lightening had hit him. He thought I was puking over his shoulder. I calmly looked at him and said, "I'm okay". At the end of the autopsy, I couldn't resist. I said to him, "You know the sight of all that meat made me hungry...how about we go for a burger?"

Finger Lick'n Good

As I recall, his name was Roger and he was a Pathologist's Assistant. We called those guys "Choppers". He would prepare the body for the autopsy, removing and cataloging any clothing or articles of potential evidentiary value. Then, on the instruction of the Pathologist, he made the preliminary incisions to begin the procedure.

Roger was good at what he did and obviously enjoyed his work. He also had a dark sense of humour. If Roger discovered that one of the young Constables present had never witnessed an autopsy before, he gave them his trademark treatment. Roger would be happily working away inside "the canoe" (the open body cavity) making sure that his victim's gaze was held captive by the procedure.

At the proper moment, when young Constable Whatshisname was distracted by something, Roger turned his back and removed his rubber gloves. Quickly donning another clean pair, if he was lucky, he was able to turn around before the Constable noticed. Constable Greengills then saw Roger slowly lick each of his fingers, one at a time, all the while saying, "Mmmmm Ymmmm."

The No-Zone

You know, it's been my experience that you can arrest someone for armed robbery, trafficking in narcotics, or even murder and have less trouble than when you give out a simple parking ticket.

I was present when Chief Mike Blake of the Redcliff Town Police was confronted by a citizen who was irate over receiving a tag for parking in the "no-zone layer". Mike listened patiently for what seemed to be an eternity, allowing the man to vent his rage over the five-dollar ticket. Finally, the man was almost breathless, like a runner at the end of a race when he said, "And do you know HOW LONG I WAS PARKED THERE?" Mike calmly looked the man in the eye and said, "Obviously long enough."

Now Mary Denney took a more direct approach. Mary was one of our civilian employees. At a later date, another disgruntled customer came to our front counter. He began a profane verbal tirade about the parking ticket, the officer who issued the ticket, the officer's parents and their dog. "I was parked outside the fucking Post Office for three fucking minutes and when I fucking came out that fucking Cop was writing me this fucking ticket". Well, you get the picture.

Mary looked at him and said in her sweetest voice, "I don't have time for this, do you want to pay the fucking thing or don't you?" Buddy laid a crisp five-dollar bill on the counter.

Respect

Many new Canadians fear the Police, their memories of abuse by the law in their homelands still fresh in their minds. Others learn rapidly to regard the Police as many homegrown

Canadians do, with a mixture of disdain or apathy. But some new Canadians have learned to love everything about their new Country, including their neighborhood cop.

Mr. S. probably came to Canada from Eastern Europe in the late 1950's. Here he found work, got married, and started a family. Life was good and his Certificate of Canadian Citizenship was proudly displayed in a frame on the living room wall of his own home.

One night my partner and I were patrolling the streets when we came upon a young girl wandering about aimlessly. It was Mr. S's fifteen-year-old daughter. "What are you doing out at three in the morning?" I asked. The slightly inebriated girl replied in a surly tone, "Nothin!" That reply and the odor of alcohol earned her a free ride home to her parents. We telephoned ahead to let Mr. S know that we had located his daughter and yes, he would be waiting for us to arrive.

The drive took about ten minutes. When we arrived Mr. S met us at the door. It had been obvious from his voice during our earlier telephone call, and from the look of his tired face that we had woke Mr. S. from a deep sleep. Nevertheless, this man rose from bed and got dressed to meet the Police who were coming to his house. He wore a crisp white shirt, a tie, and dress pants. He invited us into his home without hesitation and listened intently to every word we said. When we left, he thanked us and shook our hands. Respect Mr. S., respect!

Can I Watch?

Early in the morning, during one long night shift my partner, Brian Roberts, and I were having a coffee break at the local truck stop. It was a rare quiet night for us and there were few customers in the restaurant. Without many tables to serve, the two waitresses busied themselves cleaning and restocking their front-of-house work area.

As one of the girls mopped the floor, the other called out loudly to her co-worker from across the room, "I'm going in the back to get bread." I didn't even think. It just blurted out. I said, "Can I watch?"

Tiller We Meet Again

I didn't witness this event; I just read the Police report. I wish I had seen it though. It concerned two of our more colorful characters. Constable Kettles and Norbert.

Constable Kettles was one of several members who came to our Police Department straight from the British Army. He was full of...colorful stories. He held many of those stories in a bucket full of holes. Norbert was a local man who earned a reputation for being odd, and had a long record of contacts with Police.

One day Constable Kettles saw Norbert staggering down the street pushing a running rototiller. Norbert was obviously drunk. Kettles obviously didn't quite understand the drinking and driving laws of Canada. He thought that, seeing as Norbert was drunk and operating a motorized implement, in this case the rototiller, Norbert deserved to be arrested for impaired operation of a motor vehicle. Norbert disagreed, not because he understood the law better than Kettles ...just because he disagreed. He chased after Kettles with his rototiller, both of them on foot, down the street and then, back and forth across the freshly mown lawn of the Police station. The tiller's trail told the tale.

Constable Kettles finally subdued Norbert and proudly arrested him for Impaired Operation of a Rototiller. He was very disappointed when he learned that the charge was headed for the toilet. No worries, as Norbert often presented us with many legitimate opportunities for a lawful arrest.

Will You Be Comin' Easy?

My neighbor, and now a very good friend, was a mountain of a man. When this incident occurred, Don Barabe was probably a strapping 29-year-old, 6-foot-five-inch, muscular 350-pound teddy bear. That's his nickname, "The Bear". I was about 24 years old, 5-foot-nine-inch, with no muscles bulging from my wiry 147 and one-half-pound frame. We've both since matured and as a result I've gained weight and he has lost it.

Don had become a wanted felon. He had received a parking ticket that hadn't been paid. A Province-Wide Warrant was issued for his arrest. I knew that he worked long hours and was away from his family for weeks at a time. Not wanting him to be arrested in "East Jockstrap, Alberta", I saved the warrant in my desk to prevent it from being entered on the National computer system. At an opportune time, a Sunday, I went to his house. We knew each other casually, and hadn't yet had our long friendship forced upon us by our mutual friend, then Chief of Police, Mike Blake. That, and the fact that we lived almost next door to each other, caused me some concern. I didn't know how he would react when I tried to arrest this big man.

I rang the bell and he came to the door. I looked at the huge man before me and breathlessly sputtered, "You've got an unpaid parking ticket...there's a warrant out for your arrest...are you going to come easy...or do I have to come back later?" I think I caught him off-guard with my approach. Don laughed and said, "Yes, I'll be coming easy, but my wife was supposed to have paid that ticket". On the way to the Medicine Hat Police station, he rode in the front seat along with me. We chatted about cop stuff and played with the radar set.

Then we got to the Medicine Hat Police station. The on-duty Sergeant that day was Bill "Pooky" Graves. I've often told people, "I'm on the low end of the tall scale", but "Pooky" was even shorter of stature. As much as I always liked and respected Sergeant Graves, he reminded me of a garden gnome. I explained to "Pooky" that I had arrested my neighbor on the outstanding parking ticket warrant. He told me that the Justice of the Peace had just left the building, and that my neighbor was going to have to cool his heels in jail for a few hours.

I said, "That wouldn't be a good idea, he's a bit claustrophobic and might rip one of those metal bunks off the wall". "Pooky" was never intimidated by big men. He looked squarely at my neighbor but said to me, "Well then, we'll just have to get someone in to weld it back on".

I quickly pulled "Pooky" aside and explained that Don was a really, really, good guy and that I had PERSONALLY promised him that it wouldn't take long to deal with this. Much sucking up later, Sergeant Graves agreed to call the JP back to the station to square away the warrant.

The ride back was very quiet. Hardly a word was said. We parted company and as I recall, Don shook my hand. Later though, after we became good friends, my new buddy always enjoyed telling the tale to everyone who was there, about the day I saved his bacon from that tough little Sergeant who wanted to throw his ass in jail.

That's One Fine Auto-mobile

Chris was a Redcliff Town Police Constable. His personal car in the late seventies was a maroon six or seven-year-old Pontiac or Chev or some such GM product. One day he visited a used car lot in Redcliff, Alberta. A father and his son ran the lot. Chris was just looking.

The son gave Chris the keys to a powder blue newer model Buick. "Take her for a spin" he said. Chris returned about an hour later and said that, yes it was a fine car. The son turned up the heat and Chris became uncomfortable. After all, he was just looking. Finally, Chris said that he wasn't in the market for a new car that day. Chris scanned the lot.

"Where's my car?" he asked.

"I sold it" said the son.

He explained that a couple from Saskatchewan had been traveling through the area when their car was totaled in an accident. They had been calling the insurance adjuster relentlessly for days. Finally, the exasperated adjuster telephoned the son and said, "Give them anything on your lot up to X amount of dollars.... just get these people off my back". There was one car on the lot that fit the bill perfectly and it belonged to Chris. He gave it to the people from Saskatchewan without Chris's permission.

Now Chris could have made life very difficult for the dealership, but the one thing he admired was a man with "balls" and the son certainly had hung his cojones out for all to see on this deal. He offered Chris the newer Buick for a price that was unbelievable. Chris accepted and signed on the dotted line.

Blessed Are the Peacemakers

I'm sure that I'm not the first Police Officer to say this, nor will I be the last.

Priests drive cars. Some Priests drive cars faster than the posted speed limit. Occasionally they get caught speeding by Policemen. Policemen also tend to have a soft spot in their hearts for Priests, Nurses, Firefighters, Paramedics and others who share in our task of protecting people from themselves.

So, Father Whatshisname didn't get a ticket from me for doing seventy in a fifty zone. But with a smirking admonition I handed him back his licence and said, "Go forth and sin no more".

Buddy

Buddy was just a nasty, mean-spirited dog owned by some of our regular clientele. Buddy could usually be found lazing around in his yard or with his head stuck in some neighbor's garbage can.

And Buddy hated cops. Any Policeman that had to go to Buddy's yard to speak to his owners soon learned to do "The Buddy Two-Step". This involved walking casually down the sidewalk past the dog. Forget trying to make friends with this big, shaggy grey and white sheep dog. Buddy would lay there waiting in ambush. He feigned sleep through squinted yellow eyes until you passed and then would strike out and deliver a vicious bite to your ankle. So, we all learned "One step past the dog, two steps past the dog, spin and KICK!"

Early one summer morning I was riding as a passenger in a Police car driven by another Constable. We were in the center of town when Buddy showed himself, far from his own turf. My partner swung the car around and started chasing Buddy. He assured me that he wasn't going to hit the dog...just give him a taste of his own medicine. Buddy took off down the street like a rocket with us in hot pursuit. We got about half a block before the panicked dog had a brainstorm. He ran up onto the sidewalk. As he slowed to a trot, I could almost see a smirk on his shaggy, doggy face.

This was the main, downtown avenue in Redcliff and the sidewalks in that area were almost wide enough to accommodate a Police car, even if you had to swerve to avoid the odd signpost or planter. My partner wasn't about to let Buddy off that easy so up we went. Gleefully, we chased Buddy for about another half a block before he managed to squeeze himself between a dumpster and a convenience store to make his escape.

I wish I could say that Buddy learned his lesson that morning, but you can't always teach an old dog new tricks. We still had to do the "Buddy Two-Step" at his house, but at least we had our "kick at the cat...um, dog".

Skippy

Coyotes are beautiful, intelligent creatures. I remember being parked in my Police car very early one summer morning. The sun was just rising over Redcliff and I saw what I initially thought was a German Shepherd dog walking down the middle of the wide avenue towards me. As the animal came alongside my car it sat down on the road beside my car. I looked out my open window and realized that this was no dog, it was a coyote. I didn't move and made no noise. We stared at each other for about half a minute. Having satisfied his curiosity, the coyote continued on.

Unfortunately, these animals can also be a pest. In those years where food is scarce or their numbers are high, coyotes will attack and kill farm animals and household pets.

One such year I was off duty and deer hunting with a friend. Earlier that day we had been stopped by one of the local Fish and Game officers. The officer knew us both and asked if we had lots of ammunition. When we replied that we had each brought a sufficient quantity he asked us to shoot any coyote we saw. That year their numbers were very high and many local farmers were complaining about losses of livestock.

We were returning home after filling our deer tags when my friend spotted a coyote about 300 yards away. He stopped the truck and we walked into the field a short distance. I sighted my 30.06 Browning and fired a shot. A small cloud of snow sprayed up about three feet behind the startled coyote. A second shot and this time my range was right on but the windage was off about a foot to the right. The confused animal spun around and hopped in the air at the same time. My friend just shook his head in disgust and brought his rifle to bear. It was over with a single shot. We inspected the animal and found that it was badly diseased with the Mange. His shot had been merciful.

Back home we were met by my friend's elderly parents who came to view our harvest. He began to tell the tale of the days hunt when I jumped in. I told them about the wildlife officer's request and how I had tried twice to hit the coyote. I proudly bragged about how their son had hit the mark with an off-the-shoulder shot at 300 yards. Then I told them how we had inspected the animal, but changed the story ever so slightly. I said, "Well Mom, we drove up there and darned if that "coyote" didn't have a collar on it with a tag that said "Skippy". Mom was shocked and began to reproach her son. My friend then spent several anxious minutes explaining that "No Mom", he had not shot some farm boy's pet, and "Yes Mom", he was sure that it was a coyote, and "Mom, you know Dave is an asshole!"

The Duke of Redcliff

Shortly after my first son was born, I heard then Chief of the Redcliff Town Police, Mike Blake, book out-of-service on the radio, and at my address. Minutes later, he radioed me to say, "I just dropped off a present for Adam". I had a feeling about what that present might be and asked, "How many legs does it have?" Mike chuckled as he replied, "Every boy needs a dog" and told me to go home and meet "Duke".

I was met at the door by my wife, who was holding a black Lab puppy. Duke turned out to be a very intelligent dog as well as an excellent babysitter to our son and his little brother who followed later. He also liked to go on Safari occasionally and that often resulted in some mischief on his part.

Mary Denney would eventually become one of our dispatcher-stenos but at that time she was employed as the Redcliff Dogcatcher. She soon had the opportunity to introduce herself to Duke and the two took to each other. Many times, we would see Duke ambling down the alley towards home, with Mary following slowly behind in the Dogcatcher's truck, just to make sure he got where he belonged. When she did need to put him in the truck, she said that Duke always rode up front in the cab with her. Mary once told me she sometimes used Duke for bait when she was having trouble nabbing a skittish dog. He would play with the other dog until she could get close enough to slip on a leash.

One day Mary brought Duke home and was laughing as she told us of his latest adventure. A homeowner was spreading topsoil in his front yard in preparation to lay sod. He had just got the black top perfectly level when a black Lab trotted right down the middle of his yard and laid down on the cool loam. The man yelled at the dog and tried to chase it off. Now there were dog tracks and homeowner tracks in the once even soil. Duke thought this was great fun and darted back and forth across the yard with the homeowner in pursuit, scarring the landscaping in the process. Finally, the man gave up and called the Dogcatcher, who assured him the mutt would not run across his yard again. He must have marveled at the ease with which she captured that damn dog.

Flux Capacitor

In 1977, I started as a young Constable with the Town of Redcliff Police Department. We had a Chief, a Sergeant and four Constables. We also had very fast Police cars. Our Chief of Police, Mike Blake, was a "car guy" and selected a fast Plymouth and a beefy Dodge Monaco 440 Magnum, which had several modifications to make it even speedier than the Plymouth. That Dodge was reputed to be one of the fastest police cars in Western Canada. It was the Chief's car, but we were allowed to drive it when he was off-duty.

Stopped at an intersection, that car rumbled and rocked from side to side, waiting for you, daring you to release the brakes and punch the gas! No one out ran that car. Until one summer afternoon when a pickup truck with no plates sped through town on the highway. He had a full head of steam and a good lead but the on-duty Constable was confident he could catch him.

The Monaco roared up behind the truck, with emergency lights flashing and siren blaring. When the driver didn't twitch, the Constable pulled along side and waved him over.

The driver of the pickup must have had a nitrous oxide kit in that truck because he pulled down on the brim of his hat, flashed a middle finger at the Constable, and he was gone!

The Redcliff Handshake

He was a hot-blooded Filipino man. His fury was fueled by alcohol and directed at his wife. Enraged, he threatened her with death and began to chase her through their house with an axe. Fortunately, she escaped to a neighbor's home and the police were called.

I devised a plan. I, the Sergeant, would approach the front door and knock. Two Constables, Miles Johnson and Dan Cornet, would stand out-of-sight, one on each side of the door. It played out like this. I stood on the front step of the residence and knocked loudly on the door. When the man answered, he scowled and asked me what I wanted. I disarmed him by offering my right hand to shake, while saying with a smile, "Good evening Sir".

He accepted the handshake and once I had a good grip, I yarded him out through the front door. That's when the two hidden Constables pounced on him, taking him to the ground. Just to make sure, I added my not-so-substantial weight to the dogpile. He was quickly subdued, handcuffed and no one got hurt.

And that was how I invented the "Redcliff Handshake", a tactic we successfully employed several times in the following years.

Chopped Liver

Every year, the Town of Redcliff holds a weekend summer celebration known as "Redcliff Days". There is a pancake breakfast, sometimes a parade and lots of fun goings-on for young and old alike. The evening adult activity of choice is the "Beer Gardens".

For two nights the town hockey arena was converted into a large tavern where residents went to socialize, listen to music, dance and consume large amounts of beer. Despite the numbers in attendance and the quantity of alcohol consumed, I don't recall there ever being a serious incident at that venue. Even so, it was deemed prudent to have the local police do an occasional "walk through", just to remind the partiers that we were in the area.

I had a slim build in those days and sometimes received compliments about my "back bumper". Now those women didn't mean anything and they were just having some fun, but a few had become uninhibited to the point where they dared to give the local cop a little squeeze on the butt as he passed. This was usually followed by squeals and raunchy laughter from their girlfriends.

After one such walk through my partner, Miles Johnson, and I were leaving the arena when he said to me, "Geez...I saw you get groped probably three times!" I just shrugged my shoulders and grinned. Miles then complained, "What am I, chopped liver?"

The Most Important Meal of the Day

In the early nineties we experienced a series of perversion crimes in Canada. People in Alberta reported finding used condoms in their boxes of breakfast cereal. A bulletin went out to Police Agencies across the country seeking information.

I had no useful information, but offered my first Crime Analysis via a letter to the Editor of a national police magazine. I concluded that this was likely a crime committed by a "cereal rapist".

The Biggest Gang in the World

A newly formed Alberta Chapter of a notorious U.S. based biker gang had set up shop in Medicine Hat.

Well, for the Medicine Hat Police Department, it was like having a new toy, don'tcha know! Medicine Hat police members considered it their civic duty to welcome these newcomers to the community. Those bikers could hardly travel a block without some friendly policeman stopping them just to say, "Hello".

Smothered by love, the gang decided to move to the neighboring Town of Redcliff. When I informed then Chief of Police, Mike Blake, of their arrival, he said, "Remember, we belong to the biggest gang in the world!" So, I told our Constables that if they had to catch up on their notes, or do any paperwork, they were to do so while parked on the street directly in front of the biker house.

At first, we saw them peek out from behind the curtains. Eventually, one of the bikers would come outside and ask if there was a problem. "Nope, no problem. I'm just doing my paperwork" was the standard response. That brought the question, "Well, can't you do that somewhere else?" to which our Constables replied, "I kinda' like it here".

They also must have been very disappointed because the locals tolerated them but were certainly not in awe of this rag-tag bunch of "Outlaw Bikers".

One night, a Probie member of the gang pulled a knife in the Redcliff Hotel tavern. The entire bar stood up in answer to this threat. Outnumbered, his fellow gang members sat down. He was sat down too...on the lap of Don, "the Bear", Barabe, who relieved him of the knife, and its sheath. "Bear" later loaded the bikers, and their bikes, into his truck and took them home so the local cops couldn't stop them for impaired driving. The Bouncer kept the knife.

After closing, the Bouncer called us to the bar. He gave me the knife. It was a hunting knife with a six-inch blade. The leather scabbard held a second, much smaller knife in a separate but attached sheath. I took both knives with me.

Much later that night, like about 05:00 A.M., I rolled up in front of "Bear's" house and placed the sheathed knives under the windshield wipers of his truck as a souvenir of the night. I'm sure he knew where they came from, but I don't recall us ever discussing the matter.

Eventually, the gang moved farther south to Lethbridge, Alberta, where they were later visited by another motorcycle club from Calgary. Apparently, that club brought weapons and left with their colours. It didn't end there. The Lethbridge Club president was later gruesomely murdered by a member of his own gang from the United States.

A Fashion Statement

The whole family was a "step-out-of-time", but when the household name was mentioned, everyone thought of the head of the clan. A former local ranch family, they moved to Redcliff when farm life became too much to maintain. They still held some land out of town, enough to keep a horse or two, but now lived an urban life in a town of a little over 3300 people.

One winter afternoon, I saw the father slowly driving on a service road for local light industrial businesses that ran parallel to the Trans Canada Highway. He was wearing his signature white cowboy hat and was driving a Royal Blue pickup truck. He was idling along, his truck barely moving. We stopped our vehicles along side of each other, driver's side to driver's side and exchanged the pleasantries of the day.

I couldn't help but notice that a horse was tethered to the back of the truck by a rope. He explained that the horse needed some exercise, but it was too slippery to safely ride.

It was a very brisk day, but the animal wore a horse hood, and a horse blanket, both the same Royal Blue as his truck. What caught my attention was the blue paint. I also couldn't help but ask why the horse was painted blue. From its hoofs to its elbows and knees, it was the same Royal Blue as his truck and the horse blanket. He assured me it was a water-based paint and was simply a "fashion statement". Being a City boy, I had to accept that at face value and we both went on our own way.

On another occasion, the man made another "fashion statement" when, on a busy weekend evening, he paraded through the Redcliff Hotel tavern, wearing his cowboy hat and boots, a fur coat, hot pink pantyhose and nothing else.

He was not generally known to be violent...well, except for the time he attempted to drive a farm combine harvester through the wall of a gas station restaurant where his wife sat drinking coffee.

On a later date, I spoke to the man on the street in front of his home. He stared at me and said, "I know you guys think I'm crazy, but look behind you." I glanced over my shoulder and saw the man's wife, holding a wine bottle while dancing naked in their front window. When I looked back at the man he was grinning from ear-to-ear. "See, I'm not the only one." Well, how could I argue with that?

Guess Who

So that particular summer afternoon one of our members rushed into the Redcliff Police station. He could barely contain himself, itching to tell of his recent experience.

The Constable had stopped a brand-new, white convertible sports car for speeding on the Trans Canada Highway. The driver was a bonafide Rock Star and a former member of a very famous Canadian band that had hit the "big time" within the world music industry. His career was still stellar at the time.

Our somewhat star-struck member related his encounter with this celebrity. He said it was "cool" meeting the performer but commented on his demeanor. He went on to say that the driver was a really nice guy, but that he was very nervous, and almost shaking. I thought, "Hmm" and asked the Constable if he shook the driver down for dope. He had a shocked look on his face as he told me, "He wouldn't have had drugs on him". Okay, if you say so.

I'm not going to say who the Rock Star was, nor will I name his band. You'll have to guess who.

The Professional Big Game Hunting Guide

I was called to a dispute at a gas station just off the Trans Canada Highway in Redcliff, Alberta. On arrival, the owner informed me that a customer, currently parked at the pumps, was refusing to pay for his fuel.

The customer was smaller than me, but his ego soon proved to be twice my size. He immediately informed me that he was a businessman and a professional Big Game hunting guide, don'tcha know. He was in the area, being a professional Big Game hunting guide, don'tcha know, and needed to gas up his Land Rover so he could get back to being a professional Big Game hunting guide to his affluent clients, who were in search of Pronghorn Antelope don'tcha know. Well, I was sure impressed by his khakis and "Boonie Hat", worn with one side of the brim pinned up, Aussie-style.

He contended that the fuel pumps registered a sale that exceeded the tank capacity of his vehicle; therefore, the pump was inaccurate. In an effort to help resolve the situation, the gas station owner pointed to the inspection labels recently affixed to the pump by a Federal Inspector pursuant to the *Canadian Weights and Measures Act*. The customer would have none of it.

When I informed the man that he could either pay for the fuel he pumped into his gas tank, or be charged with theft, he protested loudly. By this time, the gas station owner was done and had his own point to prove. I told him it was unnecessary but he insisted. The local Federal Canadian Weights and Measures Inspector was called out, after hours, by the gas station owner and at his expense. It probably cost the owner more than the price of the fuel in dispute, but he had enough of this guy. The after-hours Weights and Measures inspection proved the pump to be accurate.

Not good enough. The Big Game hunting guide was right and he intended to prove it. So, there he was, on the ground, on his back with a wrench, removing the bolts securing the gas tank to his Land Rover. The tank removed, he began pouring the fuel into gas cans provided by the station's owner. Well, wouldn't you know it, the pumps were accurate after all. The customer sheepishly re-installed his gas tank but was now completely out of gas. Had I been the owner, I would have told him to push his vehicle to the next available gas station. This owner was kind enough to sell him precisely the amount of fuel he requested, if only to be finished with him. An hour of my life I'll never get back. But that's not the end of the story.

My Brother-in-Law was born and raised in Trinidad. Several years later my wife and I were in Calgary visiting with the family and we were invited to celebrate New Years Eve with my Brother-in-Law and my wife's sister at the Caribbean Canadian Club. There were shared tables and we found ourselves seated across from a very nice Island lady and her husband. I thought he looked vaguely familiar but couldn't immediately recall where I knew him from.

As the evening progressed, I learned that he was the Grandson of a former Canadian Prime Minister. He also told me that he was a professional Big Game hunting guide, don'tcha know. And yes, he was very familiar with Pronghorn Antelope hunting in the Medicine Hat area.

It Never Hurts to Ask

Early one summer evening while working with the Town of Redcliff Police Department, Constable Colin Grant, my partner for the night, and I returned to our police car to discover a flat tire.

The afternoon summer heat still lingered yet we were both still quite fresh with clean, pressed uniforms and shiny boots. We had the jack and the spare tire out of the trunk but neither of us relished the thought of getting sweaty and grimy while completing that task. No sense in both of us getting filthy and as we tried to decide who would do the dirty deed, Colin glanced up the street.

Two men who we were well acquainted with after many arrests happened to be ambling up the sidewalk in our direction. Colin pointed at our car and said to the men, "This police car has a flat tire. How about you change it?" Given our history, I expected them to tell us, "how about you pound sand?" Instead, to my great surprise, they said, "No problem" and got us back on the road in no time.

I guess it never hurts to ask.

The Friendly Roofer

It was a blistering hot summer day and I was patrolling in an older neighborhood within the Town of Redcliff. The sun was bright, and the temperature felt like a furnace. Despite having my car air conditioner blowing full blast, I still had the driver's door window down as I slowly cruised along. Ahead I spotted a man perched precariously on the very steep roof of a pre-war house, replacing shingles. We waved at each other casually as I drove by.

A half hour or so later, I drove by again and was greeted by the same roofer who waved vigorously at me. I waved back and continued my Patrol. Some time elapsed and I again passed the house. As before, the roofer waived to greet me. This time he seemed very excited to see the Police car. I waved back and continued on, thinking, "Boy that guy sure likes the Police".

About a block later it hit me.... the first time I drove by, there was a ladder propped up against the side of the house.

Y'all Come Back Now, Y'Hear

It was well after closing time for the Redcliff Hotel bar, the last business to be open on any night of the week. As we neared the area, my partner Bill Sharpe and I came across a semi tractor-trailer unit bearing licence plates from the southern United States, parked up the street from the bar and directly in front of the Town Hall. The four-way flashers were on and the driver stood on the road looking bewildered.

We pulled up behind and approached the man on foot. Happy to see us, he quickly began to explain that he was lost. "Hey Officers, I must've got turned a 'round. I'm a lookin' for the DOH-minion Glass Factory. Can y'all help me out?"

That was the heaviest "Southern Drawl" I had ever heard for real and his words poured out of his mouth thick, like syrup. I thought his accent was awesome.

I've always been somewhat of a mockingbird and had the habit of mimicking the regional and ethnic accents of other cultures, something that is no longer appropriate in everyday life today. But I replied like a Southern Sir and said, "Well Son, you're so close y'all could spit. Now y'all take your rig north on this here road 'til you cain't go no further. Then y'all turn left onto the Heavy Truck Route. Follow the road 'round the big curve and it'll take y'all right to the front gate."

The driver either didn't notice that I was mimicking him, or he didn't care. He happily thanked me for the directions and went on his way. As he pulled away, my partner grinned and asked, "What's with that 'Y'all' stuff?" I replied, "Well, we are in Southern Alberta...the Deep South!"

I Want to Talk to Him

The Constable was a very aggressive small-town Cop. And his targets were all bonafide bad guys. He just came up a little short on the evidence sometimes.

Now we all knew that a particular young man was doing almost all the car prowling thefts in our area. The Constable made this young man his personal project...to the point where said young man had his lawyer obtain a court order restricting the Constable from having any contact with him.

A week later I was riding with that Member when we saw young Mister X drive by. The Constable immediately hit the lights and siren. "What are you doing?" was my response. He said nothing and pulled over the truck. We all bleed blue, I thought, as we walked up to the vehicle. The driver recognized the Constable and immediately began to invoke the name of his lawyer.

Our Member said, "I don't want to talk to you" and pointed to the passenger. He said, "I want to talk to him".

The passenger, Terry, was a "burn-out". The Constable separated Terry from his friend and began to question him between our vehicles. "You know what we want to talk to you about." "Uh, the beer in the truck?" said Terry. The Constable looked at me and shook his head slowly. "Uh, the stunting on 6th. Street?" said Terry. The Constable looked at me, and then at Terry. He sighed as he slowly shook his head, "No". Terry wanted to please us and offered up, "Uh, those car parts we took?"

The Constable just nodded his head and put Terry into the back seat of the Police car. A brief Field Interrogation and a few minutes later, young Mister X reluctantly joined his friend in the prisoner compartment of our police car. His truck was "stripped" at our impound lot.

Wait for the Other Shoe to Drop

So, what's it like growing up as a kid in a small town, where your Dad is one of the Cops? For the most part, my sons say they experienced very little trouble from the other kids.

Nevertheless, my oldest told me that while in Junior High School he was once surrounded by four or five of the "cool kids" who overpowered him. He was then unceremoniously thrown head first into a nearby garbage dumpster. The other kids slammed the lid closed and sat on it, preventing his escape. They taunted him by calling him a "Narc" until a teacher coming out of the school put the run on them.

Sometime later, these same kids approached Adam to tell him that I caught them drinking in the park over the past weekend. I made them pour out their liquor and sent them home, but they weren't complaining. "Your Dad was really cool. He didn't give us tickets and he didn't even tell our parents!" So, Adam got to hang out with them for a while.

Despite that the "Sergeant Dad Statute of Limitations" has long since passed, our younger son, Eric, still just smirks and doesn't say too much about the mischief he and his friends got into. Yes, I heard about them pushing dumpsters into the middle of the street and he did tell me about the time Constable Miles Johnson caught him and his buddies playing with illegal firecrackers in the river coulees, where they nearly started a prairie grass fire. Miles said, "Peskor, I'm driving my police car to your Mom and Dad's house...you better get on your bike and get there before I do."

Even as he was a young man, no longer living at home, I would get the occasional call, "Hi Dad...just checking in with my Parole Officer. I figured I'd tell you about the ticket before you heard it from someone else!"

And then there was the Cop's kid story that happened long before High School, when Adam attended a Grade 1-6 Elementary School near our home. He came home after school and was almost in tears. He was missing his first, real wrist watch and was terrified that he would be in trouble.

A quick investigation revealed that Adam had attended school that day, but forgot to bring his Library books. The Principal decided to arbitrarily take my son's wrist watch and hold it as collateral pending return of the overdue books from the School Library. Adam told me this was routine and the Principal would often take one shoe from a child and make them walk around all day missing the matching piece of footwear.

He surely must have thought that I was making a mountain out of a mole hill when I showed up at the school in full uniform. I briefly considered asking for the return of my son's $10,000.00 Rolex but took another approach. I accused the Principal of theft. Of course, he said it wasn't theft as he never meant to keep it for himself. I educated him when I told him the law considered it theft to deprive, even temporarily, the lawful owner of their property.

I then mused about me stopping him for a traffic violation one day. What if he forgot his driver's licence at home? No problem, as I could, by his logic, take one of his shoes, which I would return to him later at the Police Station when he produced the document. Well guess what? We then discussed alternatives to taking personal property or embarrassing kids at school.

Adam later told me that kids who forgot their library books now had to write a short essay about why it is important to be responsible for the items they borrow.

Radar Love

Constable Bill Dagg was a member of the Redcliff Town Police with previous experience in the big City of Calgary. Bill was a nice guy to have as a co-worker and friend. He had a sharp sense of humour and a quick wit, was generally slow to anger and never known to be physically abusive. But if he caught you fair and square committing an offence, big or small, Bill loved to "rub it in".

The Town of Redcliff sits on the Trans-Canada Highway a stone's throw west of the City of Medicine Hat. As eastbound drivers, weary of the lunar landscape between Calgary and Medicine Hat saw the City skyline on the horizon, they often ignored the speed limit reduction on the highway through Redcliff. Some drivers, eager to get off the road, actually sped up. When Bill had a driver pulled over for speeding, he often played the 1973 hit song "Radar Love" over the police car P.A. system as he slowly and meticulously filled out the Violation Ticket.

The Redcliff Town Police Chief, Mike Blake, was not averse to writing the occasional traffic ticket himself. He liked to "zero out" any time advantage a driver gained by speeding through town. I was present when an irate motorist asked, "How long is it going to take you to write that ticket?" Mike replied, "I'm making a career out of it".

2

Do You D.U.I.?

Winch Way Outta' Here?

It was a dark and stormy night.... really.

I was working a night shift with Constable Miles Johnson. We received a complaint about an impaired driver and this guy was, by all accounts, a menace. He was very, very drunk and was at the wheel of a semi tractor-trailer unit.

We found and stopped the suspect vehicle on a little used service road in a light industrial area. Miles spoke to the driver and requested that he step down from the high cab. The man that emerged was about five feet seven inches tall and must have weighed three hundred pounds. He was, as reported, very, very drunk.

Back in those days paving was at a premium in that area of town. It was pouring rain as the driver stepped down from his truck, where he lost his footing on the slippery, wet clay road surface and slid into the ditch. He was trapped, wallowing in the mud. Every time the poor fellow tried to stand up, his feet went out from under him and down he'd go.

This was amusing for a while but we had things to do and places to be so we went in after him. Did I mention that the driver was five feet seven inches tall and weighed in at a svelte three hundred pounds? Or that it was pouring rain and he was now covered from head to toe in mud, slimy as snot? Every time we picked him up, he would either slip from our grip or the three of us would lose our footing and fall back into the mud together. We were beat and we knew it.

I claim to have had a moment of brilliant inspiration. Clawing my way up the ditch and back to our Patrol car, I used our "mobile phone" (pre-cellular for you young pups) to call our towing contractor.

A few minutes later the tow truck arrived. We hooked a cable around our suspect and winched him out of the ditch and into custody. The tow truck driver was laughing so hard he didn't have the heart to charge us for the job.

Name Dropper

Michael Blake was once the Chief of the Redcliff Police Department. A reluctant Administrator, Mike liked to occasionally don his uniform and work the odd night shift to "keep his hand in".

It was one of those nights when I stopped an impaired driver. The arrested man sat handcuffed in the back seat of our Police car. He was very verbal in his protest and loudly informed me, "I'm a personal friend of Mike Blake, your boss, the Chief of Police!"

I looked sideways at Mike. He just grinned and shrugged his shoulders. Mike then informed the suspect who he was. Our man looked at us very sheepishly and said, "Well, you can't blame a guy for trying".

Grant's Law

Those of us who endured the now obsolete R.C.M.P. Borkenstein Breathalyzer training course to become Evidentiary Breathalyzer Technicians will never forget the hours of instruction on the principles of breath alcohol testing.

Besides learning how to actually operate the "machine" (I can call it that now without penalty from my instructors because I no longer practice the discipline), we had to memorize the many scientific laws and principles that breath testing was based upon. There was Charles Law, Henry's Law and Widmark's Hypothesis, and other formulas and just plain "magic" that all went into a successful Breathalyzer instrument test.

One read in part, "At a given temperature, the amount of solute in the vapor above a solution is directly proportional to the amount of solute in the solution".

Also, during the Course, candidates were occasionally given the opportunity to act both as "testers" and as real, live drinking subjects.

It was, presumably, during one of these sessions that Constable Colin Grant, of the Redcliff Police Department, formulated his own Theory, now generally accepted as a "Law" of breath testing science. The Law reads, "The attractiveness of a member of the opposite sex is directly proportional to the amount of alcohol consumed". This is Grant's Law.

3

All for Fun

Smokin'

Constable Brian Zens was new to the Medicine Hat Police Service and eager to prove himself. One night he found himself at the Police station, having been summoned to the office of the on-duty Staff Sergeant for some reason. When the call of a nearby break and enter in progress came over the radio, he ran to the parking lot.

He had no way of knowing that the call was bogus. There was no way that he could have seen the hidden video camera or the many faces peering out from the darkened windows on that side of the building. There was no way that he could have detected the slender wire leading from a metal parking lot plug-in post to the underside of his car, where a smoke grenade was attached.

Some watched in real-time and others later viewed the video, but we were all fascinated by what happened next. The rookie Constable started his car and began to pull forward. Seconds later there was a flash followed by a huge cloud of white smoke which erupted from underneath the car.

He leapt out in a panic. He didn't know what was happening, just that it was bad. Enter a Senior Constable.

This particular Senior Constable, Gerald Boucher, had engineered the whole plot. He had also removed the fire extinguisher from his victim's car trunk. Acting appropriately as the Senior Member, he began screaming at the new guy to get his fire extinguisher. The junior Constable dutifully complied but on opening the trunk, couldn't find it. The Senior Constable's performance as an in-your-face Drill Sergeant was superb.

"What do you mean you can't find your fire extinguisher? Didn't you complete your car check sheet at the start of shift? What's wrong with you, little man? Find It! Find it!" commanded Boucher. The new member was in pain. The rest of us were mesmerized by what happened next.

Anyone who has witnessed a smoke grenade, or any other pyrotechnic device detonate can testify that these items tend to generate a considerable amount of heat. And most cars, even the newer models, tend to accumulate a certain amount of oil, grease and other combustible petroleum products on their undersides. We were all surprised by the sight of flames licking up from underneath the car.

Fortunately, the blaze quickly expired on its own with no serious damage and the video was not presented as evidence in anyone's Service Disciplinary Hearing.

Ho Ho Ho

She was a very nice young woman who was hired as a Police Dispatcher. She was also gullible when it came to dealing with the pranks of cops.

Christmas Eve nightshifts were usually uneventful in the small Town of Redcliff. This had the makings for mischief. The call came in near Midnight and our brand-new Dispatcher answered a cry for "Help". The call was, of course, made by a very bored Constable Dan Cornet from a nearby payphone.

"There's a guy breaking into my house, send the cops quick!" In those days, Dispatchers didn't have the advantage of a modern 9-1-1 computer console to display the address of the caller. "Okay Sir, where are you?"

"Jesus-H-Christ...he's inside my house...send the cops!" Our dispatcher said, "I need your address Sir, where are you?" "He's in my living room, what's wrong with you? Send the cops now!" This time she almost pleaded, "Sir, I'm trying to help you...where are you?"

"The guy's in my living room, he's got a red jacket on". She said, "Okay good, a red jacket...what's your address?" "He's by my Christmas tree and he's doing something."

Our Dispatcher was now practically in tears as she screamed into the phone, "I can't tell the Police where to go unless you give me your address!"

"He looks like a hippy; he's got a long white beard".

Then it hit her. Christmas Eve...Christmas tree...red jacket... long white beard.

His Bark Was Worse Than His Bite

We surrounded a house where a "biker–type" drug dealer was holed up. We had all the necessary paper work...arrest warrant, search warrant, etc.

I saw the guy peeking out the windows at us. We later found holes in the walls where he had fired a 12-gauge shotgun, presumably frustrated at being caught. He finally came out of the house and surrendered without incident.

As we approached the house to conduct the search, we were met at the window by the most vicious German Shepherd dog you don't ever want to meet. This thing was trying to eat us through the glass. We all held back with great apprehension.

Sergeant Reginald Leibel just grinned and walked into the house alone. We heard a lot of howling, screaming, barking and yipping. Then Reg emerged from the house with the German Shepherd leashed, by a slender piece of binder twine. He tied the dog to a nearby tree and the rest of us then bravely entered the house to conduct our search.

A few minutes later, Reg came into the house and announced that the dog had escaped. "Very funny" was the communal reply. But then someone looked outside and saw that the dog had indeed got free. We shared a few tense moments but quickly got back to work.

I was bent over...intently examining the loaded .30-30 lever action Winchester rifle that I found hidden under a living room chair when I heard Cujo behind me. My heart leapt to my throat and I think I was clawing at the ceiling when, in sheer terror, I looked behind me and saw Reg, laughing and still trying to bark like a dog.

An Open and Shut Case

It's not all lights and sirens, rushing from call to call. It's not all excitement. Sometimes we endure long and boring, long and tiring.... oh, loooong shifts where nothing happens.

Idle hands are the Devil's workshop they say.

My patrol area that night was about 11 square miles, mostly residential. I had just crested a small hill and had keyed the radio microphone to answer a call from another bored Policeman when I saw something out of place.

The entire block was asleep but for one house where the automatic garage door was opening. But I saw no one around the house or in the attached garage. I keyed my microphone again and told the other Constable that I might have something going on here. I stopped my car and shut off the headlights.

The garage door started to close. I keyed my mike again and said that I definitely had something going on here. The garage door started to open. It didn't take long for me to realize that this particular garage door opener was faulty and was reacting to my police car radio signals.

It also didn't take long for a confused homeowner in his pajamas to come out to examine his garage door. He looked around, shrugged his shoulders, and closed the door. I waited about thirty seconds, and then keyed the mike again. Up the door went and out came the homeowner. He looked around and again closed the door. We repeated this several more times before I decided to let the poor guy have some sleep.

I've Seen the Light

There was a tradition in the Medicine Hat Police Service. It required that any new recruit be "tested for his mettle" in a surprise situation concocted by his more experienced peers.

This meant that the recruit would become the target of a great practical joke. One of the classics involved tossing an "inflatable woman" into the College pond late at night. The newbie would then be dispatched to the scene where he would find a very convincing "body" floating face down in the moonlit water. More than a few recruits selflessly jumped into the pond to save poor "Inflatable Annie".

Another favorite trick was the B&E in Progress. One recruit was dispatched to a vacant house where a break and enter was happening, "right now!" Hidden inside was one of the aforementioned more experienced members who would, at the proper moment, leap out of a dark corner and yell, "BOO!"

Constable Jim Balmer already had a few miles on him. He was a seasoned Paramedic who decided to join the Police Service. Our practical jokers failed to take that experience into account as did the senior Constable who hid in a closet.

First on scene, Jim the rookie, learned from the radio that any backup was a long way away. He decided to search the premises alone. The hidden senior Constable, "Zaz", could tell by the sound of heavy breathing that our new man was intent on catching anyone inside the darkened premises. Just as Jim neared, "Zaz" leapt from the closet, yelling "ARRRGH!" There was no hesitation. Jim's right arm, the one carrying his long, metal, four-cell flashlight, swung out and deftly struck the senior member across the head, knocking him down and probably nearly unconscious. As his knees buckled, "Zaz" moaned, "Holy Fuck".

This was supposed to be the end of practical jokes of this nature...well, not quite.

Pooper-Scooper

In Medicine Hat, we have been blessed with a succession of outstanding Canine Canadian members. I have heard police officers from other Agencies complain that their K-9 units couldn't track a bleeding elephant through three feet of snow. Ours have been terrific.

"Basco", a German Shepherd and Brian Christmann were one of our K-9 teams. I loved Basco because he was selectively aggressive. He knew the difference between the good guys and the bad guys. Brian was so confident of Basco's temperament that he often allowed him to roam the hallways of the Police station unescorted.

Being members of our crew meant that Basco and Brian were not immune from the odd practical joke. So, I sought out our Staff Sergeant. Staff heard my plan and agreed instantly. At the very end of a night shift, when Basco and Brian were just unwinding, there came an announcement over the building P.A. system. A very pissed off Staff Sergeant announced, "Brian! Get down here! That mangy mutt of yours just laid a log outside of the Sergeant's office!"

Moments later, Brian came running around the corner, panic on his face. He looked at us, then at the carpet. He looked at us again, then at the carpet. He saw nothing on the floor and then knew we had him.

Basco was to have his revenge. A couple of months later I rounded the corner into the Patrol area where my nose was assaulted by the most ungodly odor I have ever smelled. Through tear filled eyes I saw it lying on the floor. Basco had indeed left a steaming log just outside the Staff Sergeant's door. A similar "All-Call" message went out but without the same response. Someone tracked Brian down and told him he'd better report to the Staff Sergeant with his "pooper-scooper". Of course, Brian laughed and said, "Yeah right".

Shaky

Another practical joke that had the potential to go very, very wrong.

The Constable was previously employed by the Ottawa Police Department. We quickly found him to be wound as tight as the strings on a banjo and he soon earned the nickname "Shaky".

During his time with Ottawa P.D., he once found himself in the situation that was every rookie Policeman's dream, or fear.

An armed suspect was confronted by Police and wasn't going to give up without a fight. Shaky told us the story...many, many times. He faced off against the bad guy, their guns drawn. The bad guy made his move. Shaky was faster and the bad guy died in the ensuing gun battle. He even had the newspaper article to prove it.

Now none of us doubted that it had been a scary incident. We were just sick and tired of hearing about it, over and over. That and the fact that if you read past the headlines you found out that the suspect died "in a hail of Police gunfire". Shaky had not faced the bad guy alone "in the OK Corral" but had been part of a larger force that responded to the gunman's final assault.

Another Constable and I sat in my office at the Police station. We had a very somber and serious look on our faces. Shaky came in at my request.

I informed him that we had very reliable information that a certain local criminal was about to set up one of our members to go to jail, or worse. I said we had to take care of this. I told Shaky that he was part of the team. He replied, "Okay, what do you want to do?"

I paused, then opened my desk drawer and pulled out an ancient Iver Johnson .38 calibre revolver. I set the unloaded antique on the desk in front of Shaky. Looking him squarely in the eye I said, "You've killed before, so it won't bother you as much".

Shaky turned gray in the face. This was not what he expected from his Sergeant. What had he gotten himself into? His mind was racing. He just sat there, shaking his head and saying "NuuhnuhnuhNo... NuuhnuhnuhNo".

My next line was simple. I was to turn to the other Constable and say ominously, "He knows too much", but I couldn't hold back. I broke into a hysterical laughter. Shaky didn't find it funny. As I recall, he muttered some serious expletives as he left the office.

From thence on, the Ottawa gunman rested in peace.

Military Police

I'm Okay, You're Okay

Constable Brian Roberts came to civilian policing as a veteran of the Canadian Military Police. He had the very annoying habit of saying, "Okay?" several times during each sentence, as in, "I went to the scene, okay?...and when I got there, I spoke to the complainant, okay?...and she told me...okay?" Well, you get the picture.

Even more annoying was his continual use of military jargon, undecipherable by most normal human beings. He referred to the Police Department as the "Section" and the Police Station as the "Guard Room." A zipper was an "interlocking slide fastener."

Shortly after Brian started on the job, he and I went to a house in the late afternoon. The lady of the household was on her front lawn, giving it a mowing. As we pulled up, she approached our car and spoke to Constable Roberts through his open window. She said, "May I help you Officer?"

Respectfully, Brian almost sat at "Attention." He very officially informed her, "Yes Ma'am! At approximately 1610 hours this date, okay? Your female offspring absconded with a two-wheeled conveyance, okay? And we need to interview her, okay?" The woman looked at him like he was from outer space.

I leaned forward from the passenger seat and said, "After School, your kid stole a bike".

The woman said, "Really?" and went to fetch her daughter. Brian turned to me with a confused look on his face and responded, "That's what I said."

Moss-Kit-Toe

It was the summer of 1971 and I was an eager boy-soldier in the Canadian Armed Forces Reserve. And there I was in Camp Wainwright in the northern half of the Province of Alberta.

As a relatively new Military Policeman, and a Reservist to boot, I was not considered to be sufficiently trained to venture out on my own. I was deemed to be a member of the S.A.S. (Saturdays and Sundays). I was assigned a training member.

My trainer was a tall, lanky, bespectacled Regular Forces Military Policeman from Quebec. I spoke no French, but fortunately he was passably bilingual. He would teach me how to be a cop, for sure. We left the Guardroom and checked out our Jeep, a real Jeep, not one of those tin cans they started issuing in the 1980's. It had a C42 radio with a whip antenna that was long enough to take out the eye of a low-flying duck.

We started out on patrol and my trainer was driving. He had the wheel, the map and controlled the radio. I was only along for the ride. It wasn't long before he called in our location. He had the map but I was confused. I knew we were nowhere near where he claimed we were. Soon I realized that we were headed for town. When I spoke up, he hushed me. Were we on some kind of secret mission? He continued calling in bogus locations until we were well within the Town of Wainwright. I felt like we had just surreptitiously invaded Czechoslovakia. When we reached our target, he called in another set of phoney coordinates.

As the drive-in waitress delivered our ice cream cones and milkshakes, my trainer said to me, "It's too hot out dere, and I hate the Moss-kit-toe."

Did ya' Dae Me Dad

The British Military have had a presence in Medicine Hat since the early seventies when the U.K. Government negotiated a contract with Canada to lease a vast parcel of land for training purposes. Situated at Canadian Forces Base Suffield, about 50 kilometres west of Medicine Hat, it is officially known as the British Army Training Unit Suffield, or BATUS. It is the largest training base in the Commonwealth, and is bigger than the Country of Luxembourg.

Since then, each year the City of Medicine Hat hosts five to ten thousand young British soldiers who, after several weeks of living in armoured vehicles or holes in the ground, are then paid large amounts of cash and set loose upon the City, where they consume vast quantities of alcohol and make every effort to fall in love.

Local legendary maidens such as "Judy Syph", "Becky Bondage" and "The Five Dollar Sisters" were always available to make their dreams come true.

Most of these boys behaved themselves quite well considering the circumstances, but we and the Army deemed it prudent to augment our regular Police patrols with members of the Royal Military Police, if only to act as translators for the Scots.

These fine Military Police men and women come from England, Ireland, Scotland, and elsewhere in the U.K., but once here they become, after a few short weeks, quasi-official Canadian coppers. They train with our weapons and equipment, socialize with us at our events, and form many long lasting friendships during their short tours of duty. They also ride in our patrol cars as the second man, or woman.

I was parked facing the wrong way in a one-way alley across from the Assiniboia Hotel, which was once Medicine Hat's official watering hole for visiting British troops. My partner for that night was a young, female Member of the British Royal Military Police.

As we kept a watchful eye on the some of the more raucous soldiers, I noticed that she seemed to be deep in thought. "What's on your mind?" I asked. My partner replied, "I was just watching some of these older Canadian women taking after the young boys, and I was wondering if any of them had dated me Dad when he was over 'ere' years ago".

Dreamy

Albert was a stout, solid man and built like a tree trunk. He was my British Military Police partner one night when we were dispatched to assist Constable John Unreiner at a domestic dispute.

This was not your usual husband and wife dispute, but one involving two female roommates. One of the ladies was a petite blond and the other was a very husky, raven-haired Amazon wearing a lacy, black see-through top. Their problem was easily resolved once some common sense was applied.

As we walked back to our cars, Albert and I made plans to meet John for coffee later. But before we left, Johnny and I deceived Albert by teasing that the big girl fancied him. He said, "Really?" and I whispered, "Oh yes, the skinny blond said I'm cute, but the big girl thinks you're dreamy." "Dreamy?" said Albert with a grin, "Right".

We later kept our coffee meet at a local truck stop and as I chatted with John, Albert excused himself. He returned a few minutes later with a newly purchased city map. "Show me how to get back to that place where the two girls live", Albert demanded.

Albert explained that he had left his pen at the residence. He planned to get off duty and show up there looking for the forgotten pen. If all went well, he and the Amazon would have a "dreamy" night. Despite our best efforts, Albert would not be discouraged. So, we marked the map and wished him well.

Several shifts later, we learned that Albert had returned to Base the next morning with a rather large "goose egg" on his head. It seems that there had been a full bottle of wine sitting on a shelf above the girl's bed, and Albert had been so "rough on the furniture" that he knocked the bottle off the shelf, where it landed squarely on the top of his head. He grinned and said that he hardly noticed it at all.

5

British Army

Six-Shooters

The appeal of anything is relevant to your own personal experience and perception.

We have had a close relationship with the British Royal Military Police for over forty years, since their Army started conducting training in the Medicine Hat area. Because of this close relationship, the RMP occasionally hosted special events to entertain their new "Colonial" friends. On one of these days, we were invited to come to their firing ranges to try out their weaponry.

Despite my prior military experience as a boy soldier in Canada's Reserves, I never had a "Range Day" like that before. We were given the opportunity to fire their new automatic rifles, we blasted away with belt-fed machine guns, launched anti-tank practice rockets, tossed training hand grenades, and even attempted to shoot down a big, Day-Glo orange remote controlled drone airplane by anti-aircraft tracer machine gun fire. It was a hoot.

The Brits were pleased that we had enjoyed ourselves. They had only one request. "Could we possibly have a go with your six-shooters?"

The Boot

The British Army Training Unit Suffield (BATUS) is a British military unit located at the Canadian Forces Base Suffield near Medicine Hat, Alberta. Covering about 2,700 square kilometres, it is the British Army's largest armoured training area. Since it was leased by the British in 1972, four to six battle groups, amounting to between five and ten thousand soldiers, train there each year.

Over the years a number of British Army members have visited Canada for training at Suffield, and promptly immigrated here upon their release from the British Forces. Some became police officers.

Colin Grant was a member of the British Army in the Queen's Household Cavalry. After his discharge he was hired as a Constable by the Redcliff Police Department and brought a bit of the British vernacular to the small town.

Colin and I stopped a car whose occupants we suspected were in possession of some "smoking liquor". We got all of the car's occupants safely out of the vehicle and to the back near the trunk. Preparing for a search pursuant to the then in force Narcotic Control Act, Colin announced loudly and in a very proper and authorative voice, "All of you... put your hands on the boot!" The occupants were somewhat confused. They first looked at us, then each other, and then each of them bent over and touched their toes. Stifling a snicker, I informed our suspects that we wanted them to put their hands on the trunk lid of their car.

Later I was acquainted with such terms as "fly over" (overpass) and "torch" (flashlight), but my favorite is still "the boot".

We Don't Mean to Meddle

There was a "donnybrook", a free-for-all brawl in the parking lot of a Medicine Hat bar. A number of Canadians were duking it out with an equal number of British soldiers. The police arrived and arrests were made from both sides.

Several British soldiers approached me and began to plead their case for their now arrested mates. I said, "Boys, I'm just a Constable...you should be talking to the man over there with the stripes...my Sergeant".

One of the soldiers pointed to the ribbons on my shirt and said, "Yeah, but we thought we'd talk to the guy with the medals first".

The Green One

Another day with the British Army.

I was flying as a passenger in a British Army Gazelle helicopter. We were cruising along at perhaps one thousand feet over Redcliff, Alberta when I commented to the Warrant Officer pilot that I could see my house. He asked, "Which one is it?" Without so much as pointing in the general direction I replied, "The green one". He looked sideways at me with an expression that said, "Well you're a genius, aren't you?" I immediately realized that at the aforementioned altitude we could see hundreds of houses, a considerable percentage of which were green.

Sheepishly, I guided him by landmarks until he was able to hover our aircraft directly over my back yard. "That very pissed off black Lab down there is my dog," I told the pilot. Satisfied that his numbskull navigator had finally located the proper target, we carried on.

I presume that I will never be offered a job as a military Forward Air Controller.

The Bollocking

I said, "Most of these young British boys behaved themselves quite well considering the circumstances".

On a hot summer evening, shortly after closing time, a group of one hundred or more people had congregated on the sidewalk in front of Medicine Hat's infamous Assiniboia Hotel, known world-wide by the British Army as the "Sin Bin". While waiting on taxis and saying their farewells for the night, it was inevitable that some drama would develop within the alcohol-fueled crowd. The atmosphere was fast becoming tense and the lone downtown area member wisely called for assistance.

We were fortunate that evening. A full crew was on duty including a member from each of the six patrol areas, a K-9 member, a Traffic member, a Bylaw officer and our Sergeant and Staff Sergeant. Two additional Constables, just returning from a contracted special event pay duty rounded out our strength at thirteen. It was, as they say, like herding cats, as we tried to keep people from wandering off the sidewalk into oncoming traffic while diffusing minor squabbles before they erupted into full on fights. Then someone from within the crowd pulled the trigger.

An empty beer bottle sailed through the air and struck one of our Constables on the back of the head. The fight was on and we all waded in.

I saw a British soldier pummeling another man barely three feet away from me. When I grabbed his shoulder from behind to pull him off, he spun around and punched me in the face. It was a glancing blow and I reacted the way that had become my habit since working in the Calgary City Bucket years before. I took the soldier to the ground.

As he lay on his back on the sidewalk, I straddled his body to control his movements while I did my best to touch the tips of my thumb and middle finger together...with his windpipe in between. It was a quick submission and as I applied the handcuffs I looked up and saw our Staff Sergeant and K-9 member standing there. They both had shit-eating grins on their faces and neither made any effort to assist, obviously satisfied that I had everything under control.

Later, the K-9 member, Tim Schottner, gleefully related his account of my scrap. I had been in brawls before, but never one of this magnitude. Everything happened so fast and the adrenaline, coupled with a measure of fear, somewhat clouded my personal recollection of details.

Tim told me that once I took the "Squaddie" to the ground and choked him out, I gave him what the Brits referred to as a "bollocking", a serious verbal reprimand. Apparently, we were nose-to-nose when I said in a most menacing tone, "I-AM-A-CANADIAN-POLICE-OFFICER and if you attempt to strike me again, WHEN you wake up in hospital, you will be taken to jail WHERE you will remain for a very, very long time". He said the response I received was "Oh Gawd Sir, I'm sorry Sir, I didn't know who you were Sir, Please Sir".

We hauled off our catches to cells and my man was booked for drunkenness. He wasn't charged with assaulting a Police Officer because I truly believed he didn't know who I was when he lashed out. Our member who had been struck by the beer bottle suffered no serious injury.

6

Court

If You Don't Know, Don't Ask

The trial was set in the Courtroom of Judge Hatfield in Great Falls, Montana. The accused stood charged with trafficking substantial quantities of cocaine from the United States into Canada. After a successful Joint Forces Operation involving Police agencies from both sides of the border, our Canadian officers were giving testimony in a U.S. Court.

Counsel for the Defence vigorously objected to the introduction into a U.S. trial, of wiretap evidence obtained in Canada pursuant to a Canadian wiretap authorization. Judge Hatfield had only one question. He asked then Medicine Hat (MHPS) Constable Earl, "Was this wiretap order legal in Canada?" Gord Earl said, "Yes Sir". Judge Hatfield then concluded, "Well, if it's legal in Canada, it's gotta' be legal here". The evidence was allowed.

But the real star of the show was a member of the U.S. arrest team. When Counsel for the Defence asked him, "Sir, did you point an M-16 rifle at my client's head?" the officer calmly replied, "No Sir". Again, Counsel for the Defence pressed the question and said, "I remind you Sir, you're under Oath...now, did you, or did you not, point an M-16 rifle at my client's head?" Again, the Officer replied, "No Sir".

That line of questioning was soon abandoned and the Officer finished his testimony. He left the stand, and as he walked from the Courtroom, he said to Counsel for the Defence, in a barely audible whisper... "It was an AR-15".

Agent Earl

Same trial in the U.S.

Sergeant Don Kyllo, who would later become Chief of the Medicine Hat Police Service, was laughing at Gord Earl. Gord had been informed that he was first up on the stand the next morning. That meant that Gord had to be prepared and fresh, so he could not take part in the festivities planned for that evening. Don rubbed it in.

The next morning, Gord took the stand. He quickly found out that courtroom procedures are different in the U.S. from what we are used to in Canada. For one thing, in Canada, you stand as you give your testimony, no matter how long it takes. The Americans allow you to be seated in a nice, comfy chair. In Canada, you may refresh your memory from your notes. You may request permission from the Judge to review that portion of your notes that pertains to the specific area of questioning. You then put the notes away and give your testimony. In that U.S. Court, you could read, verbatim, from your Police report. They also referred to Gord as "Agent Earl". Kinda' sounds like something that should be sprayed on jungle foliage to reveal enemy bunkers. Gord finished his testimony and left the Courtroom when he saw Don studying his notes.

"You may as well put those away...they don't allow you to review your notes in Court down here", said Gord. Don turned green. Suddenly he regretted those last few rums from the party the night before. In a panic, he ran to the washroom, where he sat in a most undignified position, sweating profusely and frantically cramming details from his notebook.

For the sake of the case, "Agent Earl" eventually let Don off the hook in time to regain his composure.

Bernie the Budgie

I had been a Policeman for one month when I attended my first fatal shooting. It had occurred at a house party. A teenaged boy was fooling around with a rifle and accidentally shot and killed another boy.

I was assigned to maintain continuity of the crime scene. I sat there all night long, alone. My only company was the loud ticking of a mantle clock and the body of the deceased. The experience was creepy.

At about 05:00 a.m. the sun started to rise and shine through the curtains on the windows. I was struggling to stay awake. Suddenly a loud screech came from behind me. I nearly jumped out of my shorts! I leapt from the stiff-backed kitchen chair that had been assigned for me to sit in and spun around, bringing my .357 Magnum service revolver to bear on the threat.

There behind me was a birdcage on a floor stand. I had been so focused on the events of the evening that I had failed to notice the bird in the room. Bernie the Budgie announced his awakening to the first rays of the sun and I almost ventilated him.

Drug Store Photos

That same matter later went to trial, with the teenager being charged with Criminal Negligence Causing Death.

Our facilities at the time were primitive by modern standards. I was the only Member of our tiny Police Department that had any real experience with photography...and I had my own darkroom at home. Ansel Adams had nothing to fear from me. I made and processed what I considered to be "amateur hobby" photographs. Nevertheless, the Police Chief assigned me and my Canon to photograph the Crime Scene. I made eighty-five black and white photographic images of that scene. Seventy-four photographs were acceptable. Of those remaining seventy-four, the Crown decided to introduce just eleven into evidence.

Counsel for the Defence questioned the numbers. "You took eighty-five photos, but only eleven are being entered into evidence?" The Prosecutor immediately rose to explain that while only eleven were being submitted, the Crown would gladly submit the remaining photos for the benefit of the Defence. A lot were duplicates. I tried to explain why some of the photos were unsuitable for use in the Court. The Defence was unrelenting until the Judge called a stop to it.

He said, "Look, I go on vacation and I take a bunch of pictures and when we get home, my wife takes the films to the drug store to get them developed. When we get them back, not all of my pictures turn out!" My eleven best photos were accepted as exhibits in this case.

Git' a Rope

The Medicine Hat Chief Crown Prosecutor (now retired Provincial Court Judge) Darwin Greaves was always an "orator". His eloquent summations from the soapbox usually left one longing for justice, if not a sturdy length of rope. After all, this is cattle-country.

I recall one summation in particular. Darwin stood up in front of the Court and said to the Judge, "Your Honour, jail is too good for this man...he belongs in the Dog Pound!"

I Could've Been a Lawyer

I had crafted a search warrant. After carefully researching the "flavors of the day", I included what I thought was the necessary information, worded in a plain English that all could understand. I had been taught to write a warrant so you could hand it to the next person you met walking down the street and they would, after reading it, understand why you were there and what you were looking for. But I was a bit insecure so I called up the local Crown's office.

I read, verbatim, the information to obtain the search warrant to the Prosecutor with whom I was speaking and he instructed me to make certain corrections. He said that I needed to use terminology that would more clearly reflect the law in terms familiar to the Courts. I amended my Information and Warrant as per his instruction and then went to the Court House to have them sworn and signed.

On my way in, Chief Crown Prosecutor (now retired Provincial Court Judge) Darwin Greaves saw the package I was clutching near to myself. He said, "What have you there?" and "Let's have a look at that". Seated in his office, Darwin leaned back in his chair with his glasses propped at the end of his nose, as was his habit and read my documents. When he had finished, he rolled his eyes and said, "Jesus H. Christ...when are you guys going to learn to quit trying to use all this legalese bullshit!", a phrase that has stuck with me since. I gratefully accepted his changes without excuse and he arranged to have one of the Court Clerks type up new documents, which were surprisingly similar in concept to my original attempt.

The Warrant was signed by the Judge and as I left the Court House I thought, "I could've been a lawyer".

Bring on the Cat

A Joint Forces Operation, comprised of members of the Medicine Hat Police and the R.C.M.P., executed a search warrant at a Medicine Hat residence. A large quantity of marijuana was seized. Two persons were arrested and charged with possession for the purpose of trafficking. The exhibits were stored in the Provincial Court house vault pending criminal proceedings.

When the JFO Unit went to claim their drug exhibits for the preliminary hearing, a shocking discovery was made. The boxes containing the exhibits were leaking marijuana as the clerk brought them to the counter. Checking inside the boxes, police found everything had been chewed by mice. The baggies of drugs, the markings on the bags and the vital "Certificates of Analysis" had the most important parts eaten right out of them. The case was lost and the JFO Unit was enraged.

Phone lines at the Justice Department office in the Provincial Capital City of Edmonton lit up with calls from Medicine Hat. The Justice Department staff tried to calm things down and guaranteed such an incident would never happen again. The next day the Federal Drug Prosecutor in Medicine Hat received a memorandum from a Court House staff member which read:

SUBJECT: Regina vs. Herrick, or, Ode to Prosecutor
"Oh, the Pot was stored in the courthouse vault
And the vault was closed for the night,
When out of a hole came a little brown mouse
To dance in the pale moonlight.
He ate up the Pot(exhibit #1) and the certificate of
Analyses (exhibit #2) and exhibits #3 through 33 in the
Courthouse vault.
And in the vault he sat,
And all through the night you could hear him shout,
"Bring on the goddam cat!"

(excerpt from the MHPS Website - With permission of Chief of Police Andy McGrogan, Medicine Hat Police Service)

Here Come the Judge

Things not to say to the Judge.

Judge: "I find you guilty and I sentence you to three months imprisonment."

Accused: "Three months? I can do that standing on my head!"

Judge: "Then you won't mind serving another three months on your feet. SIX MONTHS!!"

Judge: "I find you guilty and I impose a fine of three hundred dollars. Are you able to pay that today or do you need time to pay?"

Accused: (Flips open his wallet and speaks like Star Trek Captain Kirk into his Communicator) "Beam me outta here Scotty!"

Judge: (To Court Security) "Beam him into cells, I'll deal with him later".

Judge: "Madam. I find you guilty"

Accused: "No I'm not!"

Judge" "Madam. I have listened to all the evidence and I find you guilty".

Accused: "Well, who the hell do you think you are?"

Good Morning Your Honour

The Senior Constable arrived in the Courtroom early for his testimony in an upcoming court case scheduled for that morning. He was very early as the Judge was not yet seated on the bench. No prisoners were in the dock and the usual troupe of curious spectators had not yet filled the cheap seats. The only persons present were the fellow "office professionals" who were busily preparing for another day. The Crown Prosecutor was at his table organizing his files to coincide with the morning docket. Across the aisle stood a couple of defence lawyers who were chatting as they waited for the show to start. Court Clerks buzzed around making sure everything was "just so" and the courtroom security guy was stifling a yawn.

As the Constable walked toward the front of the courtroom, a vestige of the previous evening announced the new day. Maybe it was the chili he had eaten last night or maybe it was the beer, perhaps both. Whatever the source, what happened next caught everyone's attention.

It sounded like a steam locomotive roaring down the tracks. The noise filled the cavernous court room, finally culminating in a low, slow hiss as that particular valve closed. An invisible gaseous cloud of flatulence hung in the air.

Dave Peskor

The Crown Prosecutor and the defence lawyers stood stunned. The Court Clerks were horrified. The Senior Constable remained expressionless.

He paused as he gazed at the vacant bench, finally stating in a loud, clear voice, "Oh...Good morning Your Honour."

Make Me Look Like a Star

Constable Glen "Wimpy" Wagner ran the Medicine Hat Police Service Court Detail like a well-oiled clock. Every day, the Crown Prosecutors relied on Wimpy to have our files prepared and ready for Court. He did not disappoint. After years of experience, he ensured everything was "just so" with no surprises.

Glen was entitled to some time off too and so he booked a block of well-deserved holiday time. Out of the blue, I was ordered to fill in for Glen as holiday relief.

I was clueless. I was familiar with most of the documents, but the Court process was a mystery. I was given a week as Glen's understudy. I frantically made as many notes as I could. The week soon ended and as Wimpy left he smiled and said, "Good luck!".

The next Monday morning, I showed up for work. I knew I was about to go under, but I had a plan. I walked into the Central Records section and laid a big box of fresh baked muffins on a table. I called all the ladies to me and announced, "Girls, I'm lost. I really need you to make me look like a star!" They were clearly not used to Policemen checking their egos at the door and begging for help, but I was universally assured they would not let me fail.

I was wondering who selected me for this particular duty. I couldn't for the life of me imagine why anyone would think for a minute that I could fill this position on such short notice. Then

he walked in. The Staff Sergeant stood across the desk from me and smirked as he sarcastically snarled, "So, how's it going Dave?"

I still don't know why he hated me. I never had a run-in with that Staff Sergeant. Well, except for the time when we were both Constables. We stood in front of our Patrol Sergeant at the very end of a long night shift and he tried to convince Sarge that I should be responsible for a file, and the associated paperwork, even though the occurrence happened on his shift and in his patrol area. I had just shown up as backup. To his face, and in front of Sarge, I told him to "Fuck Off". Sarge sided with me.

As he stood across my desk in the Court Detail office, I smiled and assured him that everything was great. He nodded and turned on his heel, no doubt disappointed that I wasn't having a meltdown.

He missed the lesson. Show a little humility, recognize the strengths of those around you and ask for help when you need it. Yeah, Wimpy still had to fix a few of my screw ups when he got back, but, with the help of my new friends, I think I did okay.

7

Technical Investigations

A Precision Installation

A few years ago, we received a complaint of ongoing internal thefts at a local gas station. Sergeant (who would later become Chief) Gord Earl and I decided we had the technology to catch the bad guy.

With the owner's cooperation, we gained after-hours access to the property. Gord crawled up into the space between the roof and the suspended ceiling to position our covert video installation directly over the cash register...and I was in the crawl space below the main floor, where I had set up a monitor and recorder to capture the thief's dirty deeds on video.

My job was to communicate back to Gord and tell him when the camera was suitably positioned. The pinhole lens is a remarkable device and provides high quality video images through a tiny, almost undetectable hole, but unless positioned properly, there is a tendency to produce fuzzy edges or vignettes. After much repositioning I finally saw a perfect picture and yelled to Gord, "right there!" His response was hysterical laughter, followed by a loud, "Get up here!"

I ran to the main floor, where I saw the pinhole lens, and the camera...and Gord's hand, sticking through a broken ceiling tile. His comment was," Do you think they'll notice?"

We quickly found a replacement for the broken tile in the furnace room and ultimately did catch not one, but two dishonest employees.

Wilf Carter

Mick Nieman was a real Alberta rancher who just happened to also be a Medicine Hat Police Service Detective. And Mick took a drug interdiction course way back when they still called marihuana "Reefer".

Fast forward to 1999. Mick and I were both part of a team investigating a local cocaine trafficker. At the Preliminary Hearing, the Department of Justice Prosecutor somehow decided that Mick was just the man to give expert testimony on drug terminology.

The trafficker and a particular customer had been using the unimaginative term "white" in various forms to communicate their desire to buy and sell cocaine. One of the conversations I intercepted on a wiretap described the seller's plans to deliver a "White Snake" CD. The context of the conversation left no doubt that the words "White Snake" referred to cocaine.

Mick confidently testified that the accused was offering cocaine for sale. Counsel for the Defence asked Mick if he was familiar with the band "White Snake". Mick said that he was not. Again, the Defence lawyer asked Mick if he was aware that there was a "musical band called White Snake". Mick replied, "I just listen to Wilf Carter".

The Judge, suppressing a smile, subsequently ruled that Mick was qualified to give expert testimony in drug terminology (and presumably Country & Western music).

The Prince of Medicine Hat

I am trained in "technical surveillance". What that means is I am trained to break into your house, install cameras or other electronic devices, and break out of your house so you will never know I, or my team members, were ever there. I am trained to steal your car, install electronic devices, and return your car so you will never know I, or my team members, ever laid a finger on it. This is all done, of course, with Judicial Authorization.

My training lasted seven weeks and occurred at an Ontario Provincial Police (O.P.P.) facility located near Brampton, Ontario, with instructors from a number of different Police agencies.

Several weeks into my training, one of my instructors learned that my wife planned a weekend visit. We were to meet in Toronto. So, he hatched a plan and I believe he was as excited about our rendezvous as we were.

One morning Mike Moses told me we were going for a ride. He took me to the Metro Toronto Police Service headquarters and escorted me to the VIP Security Unit. These guys are charged with the responsibility to arrange secure transport, accommodation and protection of foreign dignitaries, politicians and rock stars.

Mike had considerable "juice" and tenure with the Toronto Police Service, so when he brought me in to the office and said "Boys...let me introduce you to the Prince of Medicine Hat, take good care of him," they sat up and took notice.

My wife and I enjoyed a heavily discounted "Princely" suite at Toronto's Royal York Hotel. And we went to the Hockey Hall of Fame too!

And that is how I became to be known across Canada and into the U.S. as the "Prince of Medicine Hat".

Log Rolling

The current Judicial Authorization was nearing its "Best Before Date" and we had to get our "devices" out of the local motorcycle gang's house. A few low-level club members had been running a "booze can"; an illegal after-hours club where they entertained locals for a price and sometimes privately discussed secret club business in a back room. It was located at the edge of the city on a small acreage bordered on one side by a coulee with a stream at the bottom. We decided to attempt a daring, daytime entry.

The plan was for me, accompanied by two of my colleagues, Sergeant Tim Holder and Constable Tim "the Virus" Dumur, both from the Calgary Police Service Technical Unit, to approach the house by moving up the creek bed, out of sight of anyone on the properties above.

All went well as we walked the shoreline of the creek bottom to within a few hundred yards of the target premises. That was where we discovered that the creek ran right up against the side of the coulee. To bypass the water on that side would have meant climbing up the hillside to a point where the neighbours might have seen or heard our movement. To add to the problem, our cover team reported that those neighbours were hosting a barbeque with numerous guests and one large German Shepherd dog.

So, we backtracked about twenty yards and I found a fallen tree branch spanning the creek. It was about the thickness of my arm. I took a leap and landed squarely in the middle of the branch, sinking only up to my ankle in the water before I rebounded and found myself on the opposite bank. Sergeant Holder was next. He sized up the branch and decided that it was too slender to support his husky frame. Looking around, he spotted a short piece of a railroad tie. It wasn't quite long enough to span the creek, but it was wider and had a flat surface. He tossed the tie into the creek and made his move. One foot landed squarely on the tie and it held for a moment, long enough for him to transfer the weight of his entire body onto this makeshift bridge. Then it began to spin. Now a "Canadian log roller", he held back the urge to scream as he plunged into the water, coming up for air a moment later.

I tried to keep quiet, mindful of our tactical situation, but poor Sergeant Holder saw my "shit-eating grin" and looked to his partner for consolation. There, on the opposite bank laid the Virus, writhing on the ground in silent hysterical laughter.

I, and Constable Dumur carefully made our way the remaining distance, and for the most part, remained dry. Resigned to being soaked, Sarge just walked the creek like McArthur returning to the Philippines.

Our bikers had fortified their house with steel doors, but Virus found a way in and out. Mission accomplished.

The Colonel

In 1994 I attended a training course at an O.P.P. Academy facility, which was then situated near Brampton, Ontario. I was training to be a "Tech Guy". Technical Surveillance involves surreptitious video installs, wiretap, "bugs", and covert entries.

One of my instructors, Mike Moses, of the Toronto Metro Police knew some of our Medicine Hat Police members and immediately took a shine to me. Mike nicknamed me "The Prince of Medicine Hat". I was also introduced to another instructor, Chris Murphy, who was a member of the Thunder Bay Police Department in Ontario.

One day early in the course, Chris walked up to my workstation and was admiring my soldering technique. He said, "Are you a Technician?" He meant was I trade schooled in the craft of electronics? I replied, "No, I just learned how to do this a few years ago".

Chris nodded and said, "You know, there's an exam every Friday afternoon...and Moses and I go for lunch everyday between twelve and one...and I keep the week's exam locked up in the desk drawer in our office". No further explanation was offered before he wandered off to the next student. Now I may have fallen off a turnip truck, but not last night. Chris was trying to encourage me to steal and cheat. He was challenging me to do it.

I had quickly formed a friendship with Larry, a Toronto Police Service Bomb Squad guy who was now being trained before transferring to the Tech Unit. We formed a plan. If Chris and Mike wanted us to learn to be comfortable doing covert entries to "gather intelligence", we weren't going to let them down. So, every Thursday, Larry and I would forego lunch and surreptitiously pick the lock and break into the Instructor's office. We nicked the next day's exam, ran to the library and made a photocopy, and then did another entry to replace the original, locking the desk and door behind us. We did this for weeks and thought we went undetected, although we were likely captured on hidden video.

Of course, we shared our bounty with the rest of the class. We held Intel meetings every Thursday night and discussed who would get which questions wrong on the test. After all, we couldn't all "ace" every test.

I knew we were busted when "The Colonel" came to town. Lt. Colonel Robert Doms was an ex-U.S. Army Officer and counter intelligence expert during the Vietnam War. After retirement he was employed by an American company that manufactured what was then, the industry standard in surveillance devices. Colonel Doms instructed us in the use of infrared technology. After the exam, Colonel Doms stood in front of the class and said, "I don't know if it is the small class size, or if you all are exceptionally bright young men, but I have never had a class do so well".

As he offered those congratulations, the Colonel had a glint in his eye that said, "Same turnip truck."

Fix My TV

I was assigned to the Criminal Intelligence Unit of the Medicine Hat Police Service. As part of my duties I was trained in "Technical Surveillance". That meant wiretap, covert entries, stealing cars, video surveillance, and other really cool stuff.

During my seven weeks of training, one of my Instructors, Mike Moses, then a member of the Toronto Metro Police Department, told our class, "Now, when you get back home, some Inspector is going to come up to you and say, 'Here, fix my TV'...well, I'll tell you how to fix his TV, pitch it out the window!"

I was back in Medicine Hat after the course and about two weeks later, I saw one of our Inspectors in the coffee room. He asked if I enjoyed my course and then said, "You know I've got this TV that's acting up". Of course, I immediately began to laugh out loud and he didn't understand what was so funny.

Over the years that passed, I'd gained a reputation as being the guy who "knows all about those electronic doo-dads". I was frequently surprised at how difficult it is for some people to adjust to even the simplest technology. But I was convinced that no one on the planet Earth was more technologically challenged than one particular Detective Sergeant. But as an investigator, he was one of the best.

One day this Sergeant stomped up to me and with not so much as a "hello", he threw a micro-cassette recorder in my direction. He bellowed, "This fucking thing don't work!!! Fix it!!!" I looked at the recorder that I had caught in mid-air, then pushed the "Pause" button to off and handed it back to him. "There you go, fixed!"

Sometime later, he was equally frustrated, although much calmer. He said, "Dave, my cassette recorder doesn't work...do you have another one I can use?" I quickly located the problem and then reached down and plugged the recorder into the wall socket.

8

Training

That's How We Roll

Besides working, we trained to work. We were regularly recertified in firearms, pursuit driving, and of course, self defence.

Now referred to as Arrest and Control, I have witnessed an evolution of tactics. The means and methods that are instructed change with the wind. The following maneuver is no longer taught.

During a recertification session many years ago, I was partnered up with Constable Dellrae Sharpe. It had been my experience that Dellrae was never afraid to get mixed up in a scrap on the street. I remember grappling with a guy on the street in front of the Redcliff Hotel bar. Dellrae ducked under my arm putting herself between me and the guy and proceeded to duke it out with him. She could be tough enough when she had to, but she's not a big woman.

So, during this training session one of the instructors thought it would be a good idea to teach us how, if attacked from the front, to fall to our backs, do sort of a reverse somersault, and using one extended leg, propel our bad guy over the top.... just like in the movies.... the "old" movies.

Suitably instructed, we began to practice. I was the "bad guy" and charged Dellrae. She grasped the front of my shirt with both hands, fell backwards and began to roll. But she forgot to place her foot on my abdomen. We crashed to the floor and were immediately treated to the sound of many large Policemen giggling like little girls.

Dellrae was flat on her back, legs spread wide. I landed squarely on top of her, our faces nose to nose. Dellrae turned beet red and all I could think to say was, "and now perhaps...a cigarette?"

Your Papers Please

Some members of our Tactical Arrest and Control Team (TACT), otherwise known elsewhere as SWAT, had registered to attend a training course in the U.S.A. They made the proper enquiries about the rules and regulations governing foreign Police Officers entering the U.S. with firearms. The B.A.T.F. and U.S. Customs advised that their semi-automatic service pistols were okay, but that the M-16 and MP-5 machineguns could not be brought into the country. Our guys would have to borrow fully automatic weapons from their U.S. counterparts. No problem.

Our Members arrived in the States and were asked at the airport if they had anything to declare. They advised the U.S. Customs Agent that they were Canadian Police Officers and that they had handguns in their luggage. He first asked, "Do you have badges and I.D. cards?" The guys produced their official identification. A quick peek at their guns and our guys were on their way.

The training course went well and our Members were treated no different than any of the U.S. Police members in attendance.

No one batted an eye when they saw Medicine Hat Police Officers, wearing their sidearms, on the streets of the City or in a restaurant during the daily lunch break. The return trip was something else.

As sworn members of the Medicine Hat Police Service we have "jurisdiction" throughout the Province of Alberta, and in some cases, Canada wide. Our guys landed at the Calgary International Airport and were met, this time, by Canadian Customs personnel. "Do you have anything to declare?" Not wanting to surprise anyone, they informed the Customs officer who they were, and that they were in possession of firearms. The Customs guy asked, "Do you have import permits?" Well no, they didn't have import permits, because they weren't importing anything, just like they weren't exporting anything when they left. This was a huge problem to the Customs officer. He had never run into a situation like this before. What to do? What to do? His answer, leave these strange men with their guns and ammunition unguarded and have a huddle with his fellow officers.

One of our Constables thought he could help. He asked, "Are we on Canadian soil?" The Customs officer said, "Yes". The next question was, "Are we in the Province of Alberta?" Again, the Customs officer said, "Yes". "Well then", said our Constable, "We can strap these guns on our hips right now if we want to and there's not a thing you can do about it".

Another quick huddle. The Customs Officer decided to seek some advice about what to do with these Canadian Policemen and their guns. He phoned the Calgary City Police. Whoever he talked to asked, "Do they have badges?" "Do they have I.D. cards?" "Have a quick peek at their guns and send them on their way".

In the Buttocks, Sir

It was the mid-seventies and the town still had a "drive-in" theatre. The Manager, Earl, was a friend and often allowed us to watch movies from within the projection booth and munch on surplus hotdogs and burgers leftover from after the concession closed. He also was a target shooter and for a small fee, he reloaded our spent .357 Magnum cartridges with lead wadcutter slugs for practice ammunition.

The Chief of our little six-man Redcliff Police Department, Mike Blake, decided that we should train for an incident where the entire Department would be required to respond in concert. Earl was instructed to load some spent casings with pistol primers only, no powder or bullets. Our revolvers were going to become "cap guns". Earl had agreed to play the role of "bad guy" and decided his blanks should provide some realism, with a full powder charge secured by cardboard wadding. As a team, we searched the local hockey arena for Earl in near darkness.

We entered a locker room and flipped on the lights. Nothing. But the shower area was still in darkness. I approached the entrance with another member. Nothing. Attempting to draw out any suspect, I turned on my flashlight and tossed it through the doorway where it scooted across the floor. Nothing. I slipped through the doorway, aware that I was momentarily silhouetted by the lights in the room behind me. Nothing. As my eyes began to adjust to the darkness, the second member entered the room. I saw the flashes, heard the booms, and caught a glimpse of the second member bailing out of the room. I turned to flee as well.

That's when I felt an intense pain in my lower back. I had been shot!! As I fled the room screaming in pain, everyone else laughed at my performance...until one of them said, "Blood!!!"

A moment later clear heads examined my wound and determined that I had not been hit by a lead projectile. The cardboard wadding of one of Earl's rounds had exited the barrel of his .357 Magnum revolver at probably around 1200 feet per second before it struck me. The wad made a neat hole in my denim jeans and my underwear, before it imbedded itself approximately ¼ inch into my tender flesh. A Band-Aid was the only treatment I received.

The Chief insisted that I seek medical attention, "just in case". So, prior to my nightshift, I strolled into the Medicine Hat Hospital Emergency Room. I knew most everyone and they knew me. "What's up Dave?" My response was, "Well, I've been shot", followed by a few "Yeah, Rights" and then there I was, pants around my knees, bent over in a most undignified manner in an ER Theatre as nurses irrigated my wound and a Doctor picked out pieces of cardboard from my back. My thoughts at the time? "Thank God...two inches lower and I would have been shot in the ass."

The Shoot Out

During my career I punched thousands of holes through paper targets with the various weapons I had been issued. Target shooting improves accuracy and develops "muscle memory" for the intricate movements of draw, acquiring sight picture, reloading and clearing stoppages or other malfunctions.

But targets are stationary. Eventually, our indoor pistol range was equipped with targets that moved away from and towards the firing line. Instructors could control which targets were presented by remotely turning them to face the shooter. Lighting could be dimmed to almost total darkness with the only illumination coming from the red and blue lights of a standard police car light bar. Still, it was predictable.

One way we overcame this was by engaging in one-on-one gunfights within the confines of the pistol range. Several large metal barrels were placed throughout the range to simulate cover. Our service pistols were partially disassembled and a Simunition "conversion kit" was installed. The kit allowed our pistols to chamber and fire Simunition rounds however live ammunition could not be loaded. They otherwise functioned normally.

Simunition is like a "super paintball" but the velocity of a Sim round is two to three times faster than a paintball, and they hurt!

I was pitted against another Constable for this shootout. We started at opposite ends of the range, moving tentatively and taking a few off-target shots at each other. I ducked behind a cover barrel as my foe yelled, "I'm comin' for you Peskor" and boldly charged, firing rapidly in my direction. At the first opportunity, I popped up and fired a single shot. The other Constable dropped to the ground like a sack of potatoes and was writhing in pain. I was alarmed. What had happened? Our weapons had been inspected after the conversion kits were installed and no live ammunition could have been fired.

I thought I had fired at center-of-mass, his chest, but the Sim round fell low. There he lay, thrashing about and clutching his groin. We had been fitted with helmets with built-in eye protection and throat guards. No one anticipated the need for cups.

You know, you shoot one guy in the balls and no one wants to play with you after that.

Big City Cops

Skid Mark Mommy

I worked with a fellow who was a much younger Constable in Victoria, B.C. when this occurred.

He told me he was the passenger in a Police car driven by an unnamed senior officer. They sat stopped at a red light, waiting for the green to go. Just as the light turned green for them, a very, very pregnant woman stepped off of the curb to cross against the light. The Constable's partner slammed on the brakes to avoid hitting her. As the mother-to-be strolled across the street, his partner rolled down the window and yelled, "Hey Lady! You can get KNOCKED DOWN too!"

Jump!

I worked with a Constable who came to the Medicine Hat Police Service after several years with the Calgary City Police. He recalled having a partner in Calgary who habitually fell asleep early into every night shift. He tried everything but the guy still dozed off.

One night, the Constable had enough. He drove their Police car to a closed-for-the-night shopping mall in their patrol area and found one of those inclined ramps that the stores construct so that semi-trailers can back up to their loading dock doors.

The Constable carefully backed the car down the ramp so as to not disturb his sleeping partner. Now parked on a severe angle, all that could be seen over the car's hood was open sky and stars. With the transmission in "Park", the Constable gunned the engine for all it was worth. In his loudest, most panicked voice he yelled, "Jump! We're goin' over!".

His sleeping partner woke with a start and bailed out the door, falling.... about six inches.

Want Some Fun?

Many Police Departments have laid claim to this event. I've seen it written up in the early 80's attributed to Vancouver and as far away as Los Angeles. Maybe they heard about it and it worked for them. Maybe our guy heard about it from somewhere else. But I was working in the Calgary City Police "Bucket" (City Cells) when I first heard the story back around 1974-75.

The undercover officer reported that he was sitting in an unmarked car...an undercover car, with no "cop lights" visible and the "cop radio" hidden in the glove compartment. His partner had left him alone, going on some errand.

The officer sat there alone in his car, writing in his notebook. He heard a knock on his window. Looking up, he saw a "Lady of the Evening" standing on the sidewalk. He rolled down his window and before he could ask her what she wanted, she purred, "Want some fun?" The resourceful officer flipped the page on his notebook and scribbled, "I am a deaf mute." He then handed the book and pen to the hooker.

She wrote, "Want some fun? Fifty bucks" and handed the book back to the cop. He wrote and displayed to her, "I am a Police officer and you are under arrest."

I Had a Dream

The telephone rang like a fire alarm in the Constable's ears. Finally, he picked up and said in a groggy voice, "Hullo?" The response was from his Sergeant who was not at all pleased. "Where the hell are you? It's twenty to eight in the morning!" That jolted the Constable awake and alert. He explained himself as follows:

"Sarge, I had a dream...I dreamt that I wasn't feeling well.... I dreamt that I phoned you and asked for the day off...I dreamt that you said it was okay and the dream was so real that when my alarm went off, I just went back to sleep."

Some guys have the uncanny ability to think on their feet, no matter the situation.

Horseshoes

Some guys have all the luck. "Mac" was a competent but otherwise unremarkable member of the Calgary Police Service in the early 1970's. Unremarkable except for the quantity of lucky horseshoes he had in his back pockets.

One day, Mac left the Police station and walked across the street to the bank to cash his paycheck. He was only half looking where he was going, more intently reading his payroll deductions stub. That's when he was knocked to the ground by a running pedestrian that had also been looking the other way. Mac and the pedestrian sat dazed on the ground when the bank manager rushed up. "Officer, that man just robbed my bank!" he shouted. Mac recovered quickly enough to arrest the suspect and earn himself an official Commendation for foiling a bank robbery.

On another occasion, Mac was walking the beat through a back alley and interrupted a break and enter. The bad guy took off running with Mac in hot pursuit. The suspect was slowly gaining a lead and Mac knew he couldn't keep up. In a moment of frustration, Mac threw his lead-tipped sap, otherwise known as a "black jack", in the general direction of the fleeing felon. Darned if it didn't bean the bad guy right on the back of the head, knocking him down and out for the count.

Tailgater

Everyone has embarrassing moments, but I just can't figure out why some people admit to it.

Long ago, a Medicine Hat Police Inspector told the guys about a very frustrating incident that occurred during a trip he had recently made. His vacation plans took him from Medicine Hat, Alberta to British Columbia. Shortly after leaving "the Hat", he realized that he was being tailgated by another driver in a large motor home.

If the Inspector sped up, the motor home sped up. If he slowed down, so did the motor home. The guy refused to pass, insisting on staying right on the Inspector's back bumper all the way. After some time, the Inspector had enough. He pulled over to the shoulder and stopped. So did the motor home. That's when our Inspector realized that the motor home that he had seen in his rear-view mirror was his own towed travel trailer.

Never Take a BBQ Fork to a Gunfight

It was during the mid sixties. The Beatles and the Rolling Stones had started to establish a new world order, but a lot of people from the previous generation, "the Beat" generation, or "Beatniks" were still in conversion to the new style. As a result, clubs and coffee houses still carried names like "The Blind Onion" and it was still fashionable (and no doubt cost effective) to keep these places dim and dark. The cool way to light a coffee house or pizza parlour was by candlelight, either in cheap red glass vases, or simply by sticking a candle into the spout of an empty Brolio wine bottle with the wicker basket wrap.

One night a very desperate man armed with, of all things, a barbeque fork, entered a Calgary pizza parlour. He approached the manager and announced, "This is a robbery!" When the manager did not immediately respond, the crook loudly repeated the announcement and this time added a threat, waving the sharp tines of his weapon menacingly in the owner's face.

He was not prepared for what happened next. First, the manager laughed at him. The robber was becoming more nervous and unsettled by this response. Then he heard an ominous sound from behind him, the unmistakable "click" of a revolver being cocked. He slowly turned to see the two Calgary City Police Constables who had emerged from the shadows, where they had been enjoying their lunch by candlelight....and all that jazz.

Attitude Adjustment

I never thought of him as a racist because this particular Constable really bore no ill will to anyone. He was raised in a predominately white, lower middle-class, first generation

European immigrant neighborhood at a time when the only visible minority was the owners of the local Chinese restaurant, and he was a friend of one of the owner's sons. I think that his narrow views about "people of colour" came from a fear or mistrust of the unknown.

One evening the Constable was patrolling alone when he spotted an inebriated white male walking down the middle of the road. Traffic was swerving to avoid hitting the drunk. The Constable pulled up beside the man and said, "Hey Buddy, how about using the sidewalk". The response he received was "Hey Pig, how about you fuck off!"

An arrest had to be made and of course, the fight was on. The young Constable was in good shape and no slouch when it came to getting into scraps, but this bad guy was tough. He soon turned the tables on the Constable and gained an advantage. As he pummeled the Policeman, two turban-wearing men approached the area on foot.

The Constable later told me the story at the Calgary City Cells after he booked his prisoner. He said that as he was being severely beaten, the two East Indian men came upon the scene. One said to the other in heavily accented English, "Look! A Police Constable requires assistance. We must go to his aid!" With that, the two new Canadians jumped the assailant and helped hold the man down until back up arrived. The Constable finished his story and looked at me through swollen eyes. He said, "I guess I'll have to rethink my racial attitudes."

You Just Missed Him

I was born in Saskatchewan in the 1950's, but was raised in Calgary, Alberta during the 1960's. My friends were the children of blue collar, middle-class parents, many of them first-generation immigrants. I don't recall any of my friends going on to become Doctors, Lawyers or Nuclear Physicists. My circle seemed to have only four career options, Police Officer, Fire Fighter, Priest or Federal Prisoner.

One of my friends, Bill Dagg, came by his chosen career honestly and followed in his father's footsteps to become a Police Officer. His father retired after some thirty-five years of service with the R.C.M.P. Bill once told me that his Dad taught him an important lesson. That was, no matter how dark a situation you find yourself in, you can always find some humour to lighten your load.

Bill's father passed away. Days later, a Calgary Police Recruiting Sergeant telephoned about a job reference for a new police applicant. The man had not heard of the passing of my friend's father.

The Sergeant: "Oh Hi, is your Dad there?"

Bill: "Nope, you just missed him."

The Sergeant: "When do you expect him back?"

Bill: "Oh, I don't think he'll be coming back. He died a few days ago."

I think Dad would have been proud.

I'm an Engineer

The driver of the car was obviously a business professional and he was obviously very upset at the two young Constables that had delayed him.

He protested loudly and arrogantly, "You can't do this, I'm an Engineer!"

One of the Constables dead-panned, "Yeah? CN or CP?"

Dress for Success

It happened in the 1970's. He dressed for a funky night of fun at the local discotheque. His wardrobe included a pair of skin tight leather pants. Those pants were so tight that the outline of his significant manhood clearly bulged through the thin leather for all to see and admire.

He was 'Stayin Alive' as he grooved to the sounds of the Bee Gees and ABBA. The night came to an end and he headed home. Maybe it was too many Harvey Wallbangers or too many Freddy Fudpuckers but there was no doubt that he should've taken a taxi.

After the crash, he was transported by ambulance to the hospital with a probable broken leg. An ER Doctor was present, ready to examine his current patient. A couple of nurses prepared the victim for that examination. A Traffic Section policeman stood nearby, eager to obtain a blood sample from this obviously impaired driver within the legislated time limit.

The nurses were mindful of his probable broken leg. How he got those pants on in the first place was a mystery. They could have been spray painted on. No way could they be removed without risking further damage to his broken limb. There was only one solution. The leather pants were to be cut off.

From cuffs to waist, sturdy surgical scissors sliced through the fine leather. Conscious of his injury, the nurses carefully cut past his broken leg and the obvious bulge of his crotch. Once the leather was peeled back, his secret was exposed. There, taped to his thigh, was a green, very firm and under-ripe banana.

Buffalos

Many years ago, the Beat Cops were issued "Buffalo Coats" to protect them from the harsh Prairie winters. As a child, I remember seeing a Calgary Policeman on 8th. Avenue near the Hudson's Bay Store bundled up in his hairy coat and high-top wedged lambskin hat.

Made from an actual buffalo hide, these coats could protect a man to absolute zero and possibly shield him from the effects of a small battlefield nuclear device as well. The only problem was, once inside the coat, you couldn't move.

Rookies sometimes tried to wear their Sam Browne duty belt with gun holster on the outside of the heavy coat. They soon learned better, and wore their gun belt under their coat. Some would stash their revolver in one coat pocket and handcuffs in the other.

"Knobby" Clark, a seasoned vet, and long overdue for retirement, once told me about the time he was required to engage a local thief in a foot chase. There was no way that he could keep up with the bad guy while wearing his buffalo coat, so he shed it despite the winter temperatures and pursued on, apprehending the suspect a short distance away.

He claimed that when he returned to the start of the pursuit to retrieve his coat, he found it standing on the sidewalk, arms outstretched and frozen in place, by the wind and falling sleet.

If it ain't true, it should be given our Prairie winters.

Doo-Doo-Doo

In the late 1960's and early 1970's criminal elements across North America became more organized, better armed and more violent. Incidents involving the use of weapons against Police were on the rise. Police agencies around the world followed in the footsteps of the L.A.P.D. after the Watts Riots and started to form specialized units using military-like tactics and equipment to deal with heavily armed suspects. The S.W.A.T. teams were born.

A mid-seventies TV action series entitled S.W.A.T. was popular and chronicled the exploits of these fictional crime fighters. The show also had a very catchy instrumental theme song.

Following a day in December 1974, known as Black Friday, where seven Calgary Police officers were wounded, one fatally, the Calgary Police Service formed its own Tactical unit.

One of the Commanders of the early unit was a seasoned Inspector.

I was arriving for work one dark winter morning and was walking the alleyway between the Calgary Police Service building and the Calgary Remand Centre. It was fairly well lit but if one walked close to the walls, you remained in the inky shadows. I must have been in those black shadows because as the Inspector exited the building, he obviously was unaware of my approach.

There he stood, wearing a crisp white shirt and dark tie covered by his navy blue Nomex "S.W.A.T." coveralls with shiny Inspector's insignia on the epaulets. His police forage cap with gold banding across the brim completed his ensemble.

And then he started to march. He wasn't ambling down the alley contemplating where to go for his morning coffee; he was marching. Smart steps forward with arms swung sharply to shoulder level, hands clasped with thumbs pointed forward. Just like he'd been taught in Cop School.

He marched perfectly to the beat of the theme song from the TV series "S.W.A.T." which he mouth-noted quite loudly.

"Doo-Doo-Doo, Doo-Doo-Doo, Doo-Doo-Doo, Doo-Doo-Doo, Dum-Dee-Dum-Dum-Dum...". Google the theme song.... you'll see what I mean.

We were almost side-by-side when the Inspector caught sight of me. I said nothing. I was stunned. You couldn't have choked a word out of me. The Inspector did an abrupt "Eyes Front", cleared his throat and walked normally, but very quickly, towards the parking lot.

Who Was That Masked Man?

It was in the early 1970's and the Chief of the Calgary Police Force was driving his personal, unmarked police car on Crowchild Trail when a marked police unit blew past him at warp speed. The marked police car was not using its siren, nor were the emergency lights flashing. The Chief had been monitoring the radio channels and knew that there was no emergency dispatch made that warranted such driving.

Now this happened in the early 1970's before police vehicles were outfitted with GPS tracking devices and even before the simple act of keying the radio microphone would display a unit number to the Communications Centre. In fact, it wasn't until 1972 that beat cops were issued portable radios and the old Call Boxes downtown were finally taken out.

The Chief hadn't caught the unit number displayed on the patrol car so he keyed his own radio mike, identified himself and demanded, "Who is operating the marked unit on Crowchild near...?" Moments later he received the response, "Sir, if you don't know who I am, I'm not telling you".

10

City Cells

Workin' in the Coal Mines

Gord Miskow is a husky man. Born and raised at Canmore, Alberta, in the shadow of the Alberta Rockies, he was a small-town boy through and through.

After College, Gord accepted a position at the Calgary Remand Centre and worked for several years in the Calgary City Police arrest processing area, then known as "the Booking Office". While there he verbally disarmed many aggressive suspects with his down-home manner, and physically smacked down a few of the violent ones who really needed it. But he was naïve in the ways of the "Big City".

I recall one day when Gord told me of an off-duty incident. He said, "After High School I worked in the coal mines. We would get really dirty from all the coal dust and you couldn't wear your work clothes home. So, we'd all shower after work".

I wondered where this was all leading when Gord continued, "Well, I was going home the other day and I was feeling pretty tired and sore. I saw a sign on a building that said 'Steam Baths' and I figured that would be relaxing." Gord continued, "So after my steam bath I was having a shower and this guy came up to me. He said, "Would you like me to wash your back?" "Well, that's what we all used to do in the coal mines, so I just said, okay...and do you know what that guy tried to do?"

Obey Gravity...It's the Law

I have been issued numerous sidearms during my career in law enforcement. My first was an ancient Colt .38 calibre revolver. It wasn't exactly issued to me but the only firearm in the arsenal of the Calgary Police Department booking office at the time. It was the responsibility of whoever was assigned the "desk duty" in cells that shift.

Cellblock guards do not normally carry firearms. The ratio of prisoners to guards makes this too risky. We relied on tear gas and impact weapons if the need arose. Nevertheless, someone had deemed it to be a prudent measure to have one firearm in the jail. And on those days when I worked "the desk" it was my responsibility.

The old Colt revolver was chambered for the obsolete and basic .38 calibre lead ball cartridge. It had an antique steel patina after years of handling by its keepers. Inside the desk drawer beside the gun laid one single .38 calibre lead ball cartridge and one single teargas cartridge. I was given no instruction about when or where to use the weapon.

Since I became a "sworn" police officer, I have officially been issued Smith & Wesson .38 Special revolvers, with both four inch and snub nose barrels, a .357 Magnum Smith & Wesson revolver, a Smith & Wesson 9MM pistol and finally the .40 calibre Glock. Along the way, I occasionally carried some "unofficial" sidearms such as the venerable Colt 1911 .45 calibre automatic. I never carried a Webley.

The Webley revolver was widely used by Canadian Police Forces well into the 1960's and in some places, a few years more. It didn't chamber Dirty Harry's .44 Magnum calibre cartridges. It didn't chamber the .357 Magnum or even the relatively benign .38 Special cartridges. It fired the plain old .38 calibre lead ball round.

Some of the stories about the "Wobbly Webley" are downright scary. I have spoken to one old Calgary copper who found himself in a back-alley situation where he desperately needed to knock down a criminal opponent. As the confrontation escalated to the point where he feared for his life, the Constable drew his Webley and fired. He narrowly missed the bad guy, who froze on the spot. That miscreant heard the shot, saw the muzzle flash, and looked into the steely eyes of a determined Police officer. He immediately surrendered.

Those steely eyes weren't determined, they were astonished. Those eyes were staring not into the gaze of the bad guy, but over his shoulder at the wall behind him. There, a .38 lead ball round had struck the brick wall, flattened out, and was now casually accepting the downward pull of gravity. The bullet slid down the wall like a pancake on a Teflon griddle. It hadn't even chipped the brick at the point of impact.

Obey gravity...it's the law.

Christopher Columbus

In the early seventies, a couple of Calgary Police members arrested a prostitute on a local "stroll". They transported her to City Cells to be processed for Court. I saw her. She was stunning. Pretty face, long legs, curvy figure and "dressed to the nines".

Prior to booking, a Police Matron (as the civilian female cell guards were called in those days) was summoned to conduct a search. The Matron took the gorgeous young woman into a nearby private room. Moments later, the door burst open and a livid, red-faced Matron emerged, spitting nails as she said, "You're not putting that in my jail...it's got balls!!!!"

Now, you have to remember, this was Calgary, almost forty-five years ago. Attitudes toward LGTBQ persons have since become more accepting. But back then, this was the heart of "Cattle Country" and the capital of Canada's "Roughneck" oil and gas industry. Yes, there were small clubs and bars that catered to those tastes, but to put himself out onto a mainstream "stroll" as he did, made that guy somewhat of a "Christopher Columbus", and I guess that did take "balls".

Five Star

The Calgary Police downtown "Wagon" crew definitely had it figured out. As the long nightshift dragged on, quitting time seemed farther and farther away. So, around five in the morning they would scoot from hotel bar to hotel bar, scouring the streets and back alleys for drunks to fill the "Paddy Wagon" van. They then pulled up behind the Police Station, knowing that between booking and report writing, they were off the street for the night.

It was like off-loading the Ark, as they led the pickled prisoners two-by-two to the drunk tank. Sometimes the passengers were truly too legless to walk on their own.

There was a brand of inexpensive Rye Whiskey called "Five Star". Each bottle had a silver colored plastic star pasted on the front. Someone peeled a couple of those stars from their bottles and cemented them to safety pins.

Two of the least inebriated prisoners were then offered the opportunity to become "Deputies". They were instructed to raise their right hands and had to swear, "upon a stack of Aunt Jemima pancakes knee high, I will eat no other brand".

Suitably pinned, and sworn in as "Deputies", these fellows would struggle to haul from the van, the comatose drunks to the booking office. Their duties complete, they were rewarded with a cup of hot, black coffee and an early release.

The Wind Was a Blowin'

About those "Drunk in a Public Place" reports. One of the "wagon crew" Constables was pounding out yet another drunk report, carboned in triplicate, on an old manual Underwood typewriter. They did so many of these that the text was almost identical in each report, save for the date, time, place and name of the person who had been arrested. The Constable said to me, "I bet no one actually reads these things!"

He then went on to pen what I'm sure would have been one of the greatest "Drunk in a Public Place" reports ever written. I wish I had kept a copy. Instead of the normal five or six lines, his report spanned more than a full page.

I recall that it opened with the words, "Oh, the wind was a blowin'...and the rain was a pourin'. My partner and I were minding our own business, when a male, who had obviously consumed far too much "XXX" wine (valued at $5.95 per gallon), leapt from the curb and bit our van". And the report went on and on.

The next shift, the same Constable reported to Cells, having been ordered to resubmit the narrative. Apparently, somebody actually did read those reports.

Torpedo Los

It was only a new building once, probably back when the sidewalks were made of wood and painted ladies plied their favors from horseback in front of City Hall. Since that time, the Calgary Police Service Headquarters building had been remodeled, added to, and generally given numerous coats of "lipstick and mascara". It has since been replaced. The old building held a few features that spoke of a different era of policing.

Only a few people knew about the hinge on the bulletin board in the cellblock coffee room. Find the latch, pull the bulletin board back like a big cupboard door, and you revealed a complex set of antiquated Bakelite switches and headphone jacks that allowed you to surreptitiously monitor conversations in the cell block and on the jailhouse visitor phones. That was removed after "The Charter" and "The Privacy Act" came to be.

There were also several small "secret" rooms off the "catwalk" surrounding the cellblock area. The pillows and mattresses found in these rooms afforded evidence of years of on-duty napping by bored and tired policemen.

One amazing antiquity was the old "vacuum tube" message system. A series of pipes connected the cellblock to other areas of the Police building. It worked like this. You rolled up a piece of paper and inserted it into a tube constructed of leather and some post-war type of clear plastic material. The tube was then inserted into a metal box on the wall that had a rubber-sealed door. Once inside the box, suction grabbed the tube and sent it like a torpedo at great velocity to its destination. One tube went to Central Records and the other went to Communications. It was capable of two-way traffic.

We had to feed our prisoners, and our instructions were clear. Count the number of prisoners that you have in custody and add "a few" just in case new prisoners came in before the meals arrived. After all, you couldn't feed just some of the prisoners. So, when we did our morning count and had say, fifteen prisoners... well, we would order about thirty breakfasts from the kitchen. Once all the prisoners were fed, we usually had "a few" meals left over. Waste not, want not....so the guards would all have breakfast as well.

Our jail breakfasts were the best and much in demand. They usually consisted of two pieces of toast, two hard-boiled eggs, and a couple of strips of bacon. Those poor guys in the Communications Centre couldn't leave their posts so I experimented and found that, being relatively lightweight, bacon wrapped in paper towels traveled the best. Hardboiled eggs fit conveniently into the pneumatic tubes and usually survived the journey. We gave up on the toast.

Kung Foo Fighting

The cell guard was working the nightshift in the Calgary Police city cells when two Constables brought in a very agitated, and by all accounts, violent man. The handcuffs were removed and as he rubbed his wrists, the prisoner declared loudly for all to hear, "I've got a black belt in Karate and I'm gonna' to kick ALL your asses, starting with YOU!"

The guard ignored the finger pointed at him and began typing in the booking information. As he surrendered his property the prisoner whipped a card from his wallet. It was a membership card from a local Martial Arts club. "See! I'm a black belt!" With that he dropped into a menacing Kung Fu stance and flashed his hands up towards the guard's face, while screaming "HiYaahh" or some such other nonsense. Without hesitation a big fist came across the counter in response to the threat. The Bruce Lee Wannabee fell to the floor and was laying there, his hands still in the classic "karate-chop" pose. As tears began to stream from his eyes he whined, "You didn't give me time to set up".

By the way, his membership card showed that he had studied the combative arts for about two weeks prior to his arrest.

Three Bag Monte

I was leaving the Calgary City Police building to go home after a long night shift. One of my co-workers left at the same time. As we exited into the dark alley, we saw a "wino" that we had released from the "drunk tank" an hour or so before.

The elderly fellow kept all of his worldly possessions in two green plastic garbage bags. He was attempting to sort his stuff out when my co-worker decided to do something he thought was brilliantly funny. He snatched a similar green garbage bag from the dumpster behind the old man and started to "shell game" him by switching the bags back and forth. As he stood there grinning, the old man stared at him for a moment, and then punched him right in the chops!

I laughed and said, "Well, I guess you had that coming".

What's on Tap?

They say, "what is seen cannot be unseen". Prisoners were brought to cells and at the booking area, they all received the same instruction. "Everything on the counter". In other words, wallet, watch, keys and what ever else was in your pockets. I was not prepared for what I saw that night.

The "wagon crew" brought in an extremely intoxicated female prisoner. She was maybe five-foot-two and probably two-hundred-fifty pounds. "Everything on the counter," I instructed.

Without hesitation, and in one fluid move, her dress, the only garment she wore, lay on the counter in front of me. There she stood, totally naked and proud as a peacock. She had home-made tattoos on her breasts. Over one nipple was tattooed "Wine", and over the other, "Beer".

Jail Break

During the early 1970's, responsibility for the custody of arrested persons transferred from the Calgary Police Service to Alberta Corrections. Sometimes the old Police Inspectors would come to the Calgary City Cells to have coffee with the old Warhorse Constables that still worked there during the transition process. I was on a day off when this happened, so I can only report what I was told.

It was a very quiet time, rare on the night shift and two of the white-shirted Inspectors had dropped by for a cup of strong coffee. As they relaxed and chewed the fat with the old Constables, the Visitor's area door buzzer rang. An unarmed and half-asleep Corrections Officer rounded the corner to see who was there. He recoiled in horror as he saw the muzzles of two guns facing him through the small cut out in the glass. Shots rang out and the whole place erupted into pandemonium. It was a "Jail Break!!" The "Desk" guy managed to grab the antique Colt assigned to his post, but dropped his two rounds of ammunition onto the floor. The pair of white shirts weren't armed and hit the deck under the table where they had been sitting. Then silence, followed moments later by girlish giggling.

The two young Constables that had loaded their guns with blanks had the tables turned on them when, as they rounded the corner into the cellblock they saw, emerging from under a table, the two coffee-stained white shirts with shining insignia on the epaulets.

Mental Health

It's Not the Size of the Dog in the Fight

Joe was a very large man. He had been brandishing a rifle about the trailer park where he lived and, to use the fitting medical terminology, was "nutty as a fruit cake".

My Sergeant and I, both of us "on the lower end of the tall scale", took a fellow Constable along for added effect. That Constable, Tim Schottner, stood about six-foot-five and weighed in at about two-fifty. Even he didn't intimidate this big guy.

Through the use of respectful, albeit contrived, smooth talking we gained entry to the residence, a singlewide mobile home. Things went downhill from there and it wasn't long before the three of us were forced to jump the big man. We were thrashing about on the filthy floor trying to gain control over him, when the man's dog came to our assistance.

As we rolled around on the living room floor, a Chihuahua dog darted out from under the sofa and bit our suspect on the top of his head. That seemed to distract him enough so that we could gain a bit more control. The moment the big man started to rally a comeback, the little dog would dart out from under the sofa and bite him again. This occurred several times until we finally had our man in handcuffs and safely under arrest.

As for the little wanna-be Police dog.... he was just satisfied that HIS beat was now safe, quiet and secure.

The Cable Guy

We received a complaint about a mentally ill subject who had threatened the caller with a knife. Due to the nature of the dispatch, we responded with all available members.

The suspect was holed up in a basement apartment. Our crew surrounded the building and we had a K-9 officer and his dog strategically in place.

My Sergeant decided that he and I would make the contact. Previous experience with this subject led us to believe he would not open the door to Police. As we approached the door to the apartment, I said to him, "Tell him you're the Cable guy". Sarge looked at me like I was the one who was nuts. "The Cable guy?" he laughed. I said, "Yeah...No one wants any problems with their cable TV...he'll open up".

My Sergeant knocked loudly on the door. Our suspect yelled from the other side, "Who the fuck are you?" Sarge instantly replied, "Medicine Hat News". Our suspect yelled back, "Get the fuck out of here". I looked at my Sergeant with disbelief and whispered. "Medicine Hat News? I told you to say you were the cable guy." He said that he thought the newspaper was more believable and again knocked on the door. Moments later, Buddy again yelled out, "Who's there?" To my chagrin, Sarge again said, "Medicine Hat News". The man informed him that he didn't want the newspaper and told him to go away. Sarge pounded on the door one last time and said, "Medicine Hat News...will you please come out here and talk to me." Our suspect was now very agitated and responded, "Get the fuck out of here or I'll cut your fucking head off! Go away or I'll call the fucking cops!"

I seized the moment and pounded loudly on the door. "Who's there?" was the come back. I said, "City Police" and received the response, "Good, I want to talk to you guys, some guy from the News has been bugging me".

Our suspect opened the door and stepped out into our waiting arms. He was immediately arrested without any serious incident.

Jump

The Sergeant was fastidious in both his appearance and demeanor. He could get into a scrap with a drunk in a back alley and he always came out looking fresh-pressed, with not a hair out of place.

He spoke in clipped sentences that were always pronounced clearly and correctly. He would never call Constable John Unreiner "John", nor would he call me, "Dave". It was always "Jonathan" and "David". Sometimes though, at the end of nightshift, we would hear a building page over the intercom, "UNREINER! PESKOR! WHERE ARE YOU TWO HAIRBALLS?"

That was because "Jonathan" and I were often unfairly accused of being responsible for some mischief to his office.

Early one morning, near the end of a long nightshift, we received a dispatch about a jumper on a bridge over the South Saskatchewan River. On arrival, the Sergeant found a young man well known to him. The young man announced his intention to jump and removed his wristwatch, which he tossed to the

Sergeant. Not being a trained Crises Negotiator, Sarge said to the young man, "Go ahead and jump...you haven't got the balls".

The Sergeant's next words were rather uncharacteristic of him. He said, "Oh Shit!" This was followed by a rather loud splash. Quickly recovering, he commanded from the bridge rail above, "You there, swim over to my men!" Everyone obeyed his orders and this guy was no different. The jumper did extract himself from the mud (the river was very low that year) and made his way directly to me. I handcuffed him and escorted him to Hospital for a mental health assessment.

All You Had to Do Was Ask

Virginia was one of the many names she went by. The poor woman was diagnosed with a mental disorder and without medication, she saw a different colored sky than the rest of us. Most of the time she was harmless but sometimes she became violent and had to be hospitalized for her safety and the safety of others. Occasionally she assaulted innocent people with her Electrolux vacuum cleaner.

Constable Dan Cornet and I arrested Virginia on one such occasion. We transported her to the Medicine Hat Hospital Emergency ward and waited for the attending physician in a vacant examination room. I had previous experience with Virginia so I convinced Dan to stay and watch her while I stepped outside of the room and chatted with the nurses.

Poor guy. For about forty-five long minutes he was subjected to a tirade of insults screamed at him by Virginia. She insulted his height, his hair color, his chosen profession, and his manhood. What could he do? He just sat there and took it on the chin.

Eventually I told him to take a break and I would watch over Virginia. As Danny was gratefully walking from the room, Virginia set her sights on me. She began the same verbal assault on me that she had laid on my partner. I just looked at her and calmly said, "I don't want to talk to you. Please be quiet". Virginia immediately shut up. Dan looked at me in disbelief. I said, "All you had to do was ask".

Virginia remained relatively calm during the remainder of our wait, although she did tell me about her ten years of combat experiences during the Vietnam War, her abduction and mutilation by Pirates, and about her father, the Mafia Don, who was going to kill me on the following 01 August. Despite that we had a good visit until Constable Dan and the Doctor finally returned.

She took one look at them and immediately reverted to who she had been earlier. The Doctor promptly admitted her into the hospital for a psychiatric evaluation.

Sideshow Bob

I've always tried my best to be empathetic when it came to my "customer's" troubles, especially when their problems are out of their control and no fault of their own. But sometimes you just have to laugh and play along. It preserves your sanity.

While waiting at the hospital for a Doctor to examine a suicidal patient I had apprehended, one of our guys brought in another person for psychiatric assessment. The Constable placed his prisoner in a room near the one occupied by my prisoner and me. He said that he really, really, really had to "go" and asked if I could watch his guy and mine for just a few minutes. No problem.

I looked into the room a few moments later and saw "Bob". He was a white male, about 19 years old. He stood about 5'10" tall and weighed maybe 140 pounds. At least 10 pounds of that was his hair. He was attired in a Skater mix of Sally Anne/Army Surplus wear. Bob's hair was a big, brown rat's nest. He had attempted to fashion it into Jamaican-style dreadlocks, but it turned into a multi-spiked, brown pointy mass. Oddly, Bob also tried to affect a Spanish accent to compliment his faux Caribbean hair.

I said, "What are you in here for?" Bob replied in his best Latino manner, "Dey'z pickin' on me cause I'm a Chicano, Man". I said, "Really? Como esta usted?" I just asked Bob how he was in Spanish. Bob looked at me with wide, confused eyes. Then he said, "Yeah, well, I used to speak that stuff but I don't anymore".

Busted. I suspect that Bob just wanted a few days of clean sheets, decent food, and maybe some really "groovy" medication.

Traffic

Clear Signals Are A Must

Constable Gordon Groft was doing his best to direct traffic around a collision scene. Hopefully he could prevent another from occurring. One motorist was having particular difficulty obeying Gordon's direction. Finally, in frustration the man leaned his head out of his car window and yelled, "Hey asshole, why don't you give me a signal I can understand?"

It is reported that without hesitation Gord replied, "How about this one?" and raised a middle finger into the air.

Y.M.C.A.

I was a member of the Medicine Hat Police Service, formerly the Medicine Hat Police Department, or even farther back, the Police Force. Now, perhaps our Police Station should be called the "Service Station". We answered "Calls for Service". Maybe the Chief of Police should be referred to as the "Service Manager". The Fire Service and Emergency Medical Service have gone through similar name changes. We all serve, serve, and serve.

Policies have changed as well. You must never, ever, deviate from policy unless you are prepared to articulate your actions. Sometimes it went beyond ridiculous.

There was a policy that required our 9-1-1 Dispatchers to send the Fire Service and the Emergency Medical Service to any motor vehicle accident where there existed even the remote possibility of fire, injury, or presumably spontaneous human combustion. The first guys on the scene, usually the Cops, couldn't call off the others if not needed, because of policy. If a City utility pole was scratched...they had to send out the Electrical "Service" as well.

One day I approached an accident scene in the City's south side. As I drove up, I saw two or three Police cars, an Ambulance, a Fire Rescue truck, a Pumper truck, and an Electric Linesman's truck. It looked like an outdoor Disco with all the flashing lights. Both drivers were up and walking around. There was a tiny spot of anti-freeze or oil or some other vehicular deposit on the ground, dutifully being washed away by one of the Fire Service members.

I noticed a huddle of one Paramedic, one Fireman and one Electric linesman. I walked up and said to them, "All we need is an Indian Chief and we can be The Village People".

You May Now Resume Your Normal Activities

I was inspired to do this by another police officer in a different City, but I'm sure the reaction I received was very similar to what he experienced.

I had stopped a motorist for speeding and the driver immediately became verbally aggressive. He yelled at me, "Don't you have anything more important to do?"

As I stood at the driver's window I spoke into my portable radio, "Dispatch, I'm about to issue a violation tag for speeding, but the driver asked me if I didn't have anything more important to do. Do you have anything more important for me to do?" The response from dispatch was, "Not at this time, so go ahead and issue that violation tag".

13

Drugs and Undercover

It Wasn't in the Cards

Members of our Police Service successfully executed a search warrant at a local residence. Evidence was obtained and arrests were made.

No big deal, right? Except that the owner of the premises was a local Psychic. How come she didn't know we were coming?

We Like You Guys Better

Our investigation involved the use of highly skilled undercover operators posing as criminal buyers; fences who were eager to get their hands on all the stolen, new-in-the-box laptops, cameras and audio equipment that found its way onto the streets of Medicine Hat. The rest of the team supported the undercover operators by providing them with close cover as well as conducting physical and electronic surveillance of the suspects.

Besides performing surveillance, I was tasked with determining the pedigree of the recovered stolen property. People do what works well for them and criminals are no different. It wasn't long before we discovered that our bad guys were targeting the same few retail chains over and over. They were also mobile and travelled to nearby cities to do their "boosting".

I developed a working relationship with Loss Prevention officers from several different large retailers in Medicine Hat and elsewhere. I was able to confirm that the items we bought on the street were supposed to be on the shelf in those stores, and that they were now missing from inventory.

After my third such call to the same Loss Prevention officer from a retailer in another city, she called me to report another theft. I told her we would keep an eye out for the stolen item and requested the police file number from the local Agency she reported the theft to.

"Oh, we didn't call them. We get better results from you guys". I chuckled a bit as I told her she would still have to make a report with her local police.

Beats Me

I was on days off when an undercover officer telephoned me at home and asked, "What are you doing tomorrow?" I replied, "Nothing special, why?"

He explained that he was scheduled to undergo a short day-surgery procedure the next afternoon, but had also committed to doing some undercover drug work for the Lethbridge Police Service that same night. "You're nuts", I told him. He said, "So, will you cover me?" Of course I would, and arrangements were made for me to drive him to his surgery, and then afterwards to Lethbridge, where we would "work" a Rock Concert.

We met up with the Lethbridge team. These guys were good... except for one Detective who showed up dressed as "Herb Tarlek from WKRP Cincinnati". He was told to keep his plaid polyester suit and loud tie outside unless we needed immediate backup.

I was dressed in grubby jeans and my "Oilfield" hat. I had an overnight growth of beard. My cover, if anyone asked, was that I was a pipeline worker that got roped into taking my 14-year-old niece to this stupid concert, and "where the hell is she, anyways."

I shadowed the undercover officer through the concert hall. He was on his own, unless anyone got physical with him. Then I was to jump in with all I had. Nothing happened and the concert ended. The UC walked into the main lobby of the hall and stopped to talk to a likely subject. I walked past, stopping a short distance away, within earshot, but not facing them.

That's when "Herb Tarlek" walked in the front doors. He was walking straight towards the UC but I intercepted him before he could get there. The undercover's subject said to him, "look at them Fuck'n cops...do they think we're stupid?" The UC laughed. "Yeah, they're pretty stupid, aren't they"?

But it got worse. After the Rock Concert, the undercover officer decided that we should work some "skid bars". Now if you're going to sit in a bar and fit in, you can't drink milk. The UC was having the time of his life, while trying to schmooze a drug buy out of the denizens of those watering holes. I sat alone in the saloon and watched him in the reflection of the mirrors behind the bar.

I could not drink beer that night. It's not that I got drunk on the stuff...it just made me sick to my stomach...but when in Rome. The sloppy chili-dog the UC bought me from a street vendor's cart was about to erupt when thankfully, he called it quits. At the end of a very long night, we headed home to Medicine Hat.

We were near the Town of Taber, Alberta and it was about 5:00 a.m. Everyone in the Province of Alberta knows that the RCMP does not work such ungodly hours.

Apparently, I may have been driving ever so slightly in excess of the posted speed limit. I was tired and admittedly a little bit "pissy" at being stopped.

On previous occasions I had been told never to "tin" my way out of a UC encounter with police unless it became absolutely necessary. So, when the Mountie that pulled us over requested that I sit in the back seat of his car, my badge stayed out of sight, as did my gun and I was, "Okay, fine". He then started to interrogate me.

He asked, "Is this your car?"

I said, "Nope"

He said," Who does the car belong to?"

I replied, "Beats Me." Our UC cars were wreck rentals that were outfitted with licence plates registered under bogus names or numbered companies.

He asked, "Is it insured?"

I said, "Fucked if I know."

Now I guess I was the author of my own misery, but it didn't help that the Auxiliary Member with the Mountie then reported seeing something of alarm. They whispered to each other excitedly and then exited the car, moving cautiously towards the long haired and bearded UC.

The RCMP Member approached the passenger window and said, "Sir, do you have a gun in the glove compartment?" The undercover officer said, "Yeah" and to make a long story short, he explained who we were. The Mounties were not impressed with me when they returned to the car. Before being released from the back seat, I was sternly issued with a very official, printed-in-duplicate, written warning for speeding.

The Rip

The officer was assigned to the drug squad as an undercover operator and had arranged a "buy" for $150 worth of LSD. Sitting in an unmarked car, I watched from a distance as he approached a young female. She accepted the money and promptly walked to a nearby male. He received the money and took off running. He escaped with our $150 cash!

A few weeks later, while on days off, the undercover operator was driving home from Calgary on his motorcycle. When he passed a hitchhiker he thought, "I know that guy". He pulled over and waited for the man to run to him. The UC offered him a helmet and a ride to Medicine Hat.

As they neared Brooks, Alberta the officer indicated that were going to stop at a truck stop. There the two men sat across from each other over cups of coffee. The officer said, "You don't recognize me, do yah?" When the man said "No", the UC replied menacingly, "YOU OWE ME $150 BUCKS!" Suddenly it all came back to him. This was the guy he had ripped off weeks earlier. He soon coffed up the money.

Having now established a connection, the UC continued their relationship for some time over the next several weeks, gaining the trust of the drug dealer. As a result, he was able to learn of, and act upon much criminal activity.

Rocky

So, one day we raided a crack cocaine dealer's house. Crack dealers are not generally as docile as the pot heads of the seventies. They often have weapons. We take precautions.

I was posted outside the residence at the front, acting as back up for the K-9 officer and his dog. We would catch anyone who fled out the front after the Tactical Team breached the back door. The entry was made and even from outside we could hear that things were not going well inside. There was banging and screaming and someone yelled, "He's headed for the front!" The glass in the front porch window exploded!

K-9 Constable Darcy Brandt and Police Service Dog "Rocky" were on high alert. Darcy yelled his warning to the suspects, "Stop or I'll send in the Police dog". Again, he excitedly repeated the warning and I moved closer to provide cover with my weapon.

I didn't know that when a K-9 officer starts to yell his "warnings", his dog is trained to go into a high-level protection mode for the handler. I also didn't realize that I was moving into the dog's peripheral vision. Suddenly, PSD Rocky spun about and lunged towards me. He was headed in fast and low. I didn't want to get bit on the legs, or other tender spots, so I instinctively offered my right arm as a target. He hit hard and I felt his teeth puncture my arm.

Darcy was focused on the house and tugged at the lead when he felt resistance. Rocky complied and went to his side. I said, "Your dog bit me" and he replied "Bullshit", Then I showed him my chewed-up sleeve.

Well, we arrested everybody that needed to be and secured the scene. The irony of it all was that I got bit by a Police dog on the entry and during the ensuing search of the house, I played with and fed a few dog biscuits to the suspect's Pit Bull puppy.

Sadly, PSD Rocky later succumbed to injuries he received during the apprehension of another criminal suspect. On October 16, 2007, PSD Rocky was accepted to The National Police Service Dog Monument located at the RCMP Kennels in Innisfail, Alberta. The Monument recognizes Police Service Dogs that are killed in the line of duty in Canada. A plaque on the monument recognizes Rocky as the 33rd Police Dog in Canada to die in the line of duty since 1963.

Golden

There are police undercover officers, "UCs", who are sworn members who attempt to worm their way into criminal cells or networks. Sometimes it takes days, sometimes weeks, sometimes months or longer. These are real cops who pretend to be real criminals, except they have to play by the rules.

Then there are Confidential Informants, "CIs", who may be criminals or fringe people that provide information to the police about criminal activity. They hold no special status beyond the promise of anonymity, and usually they are known in police reports only by a number. Typically, they are motivated by cash rewards, revenge or perhaps some consideration regarding outstanding criminal charges they face. They may not receive any direction from the police.

And then there are "Agents". Agents are frequently bonafide criminals who enter into a "contract" to assist the police in a specific investigation. They come with credentials, often being recognized as someone who lived in the same prison cellblock as our target or someone they know from the neighborhood.

They receive payment or other consideration in exchange for their participation. The police may direct them to pursue specific avenues of investigation. Agents agree to out themselves and testify in Court. The use of Agents can easily result in significant liability, so they are sparingly employed nowadays.

Years ago, we were not so mindful of civil liability. Our Agent had introduced the UC to a cocaine trafficker. A deal was arranged to take place in a little used parking lot behind a local shopping mall. The surveillance team reported observing a "successful buy" signal, so we moved in fast with our marked units. I skidded to a stop directly behind the UC vehicle with my emergency lights flashing.

The doors blew open! Still acting in an undercover capacity our UC officer, Colin Grant, bailed out of the driver's door directly into the arms of waiting uniformed members where he was handcuffed and hauled away. The drug dealer bolted from the driver's side rear passenger door and made about one hundred feet before he was captured by one of our K-9 officers and his dog. A third man made a dash from the passenger side door, almost into my arms.

The fight was on! We grappled at the side of the vehicle. It got intense and at one point, as he tried to escape, I almost ripped the sleeve off of his leather jacket. Another Constable, Les Phee, came to my aid. We struggled with this man, and I confess, at one point I thought I could "stun" him into submission by polishing the hood of my police car with his forehead.

Now Constable Murray Morton, our K-9 officer, had the dealer fully compliant, on his knees and hands cuffed behind his back. Colin, our UC, still playing the role of a buyer, was securely in the back seat of a police unit. Our K-9 "Thor" surveyed the scene, and saw some unfinished business. With no direction from his handler Murray, he charged to our aid.

Thor was faced with six legs. Four were clad in navy blue with red stripes. Two wore an ugly patterned polyester popular at the time. Thor hated polyester as much as I did and dove into the fray. He bit hard into the man's calf and shook his head to compel submission.

Now Les Phee had a phobia. He was deathly afraid of dogs. Drunken six-foot-two biker with a broken beer bottle, no problem. Snarling Chihuahua.... well, that could be a problem. Nevertheless, he tried. I heard him say, "No Thor!" and saw his hand moving towards the dog's head. I yelled "Les! No!", and pulled his hand back. At that same moment Murray saw what was happening and yelled, "THOR!!! OFF!!!" Thor obediently released and returned to his side. All our prisoners were then secured and transported to cells.

At cells, the dealer was on the phone, getting "lawyered up". I was summoned to an office where Colin, our smiling UC, sat at a desk. Nearby was the third man, wearing a torn leather jacket, shredded pants and sporting a couple of strawberries on his forehead. I was then introduced to our Agent. I hung my head and said, "Oh man, I didn't know" and started to apologize. He interrupted me with a laugh and said, "Are you fucking kidding me?" He went on to say that the cops would never handle one of their own like that and we had made him "Golden" on the street!

Bastards!

We were working a Joint Forces drug operation that spanned several communities in southern Alberta. Members of the Calgary Police Service and the Royal Canadian Mounted Police partnered with us to put a stop to this drug street gang that was selling crack cocaine in Medicine Hat and Brooks, Alberta.

The R.C.M.P. Special "I" section planned to install a "technical surveillance device" but needed to ensure that a specific person in the criminal group was "out of the game" while they did so.

He owned and operated a one-car taxi business, so late one night, acting in an undercover capacity, I called for a cab. He picked me up at a casino in the south end of Medicine Hat and was to take me to a downtown bar.

We chatted along the way and I did my best to keep him occupied with conversation. Not long after we left the casino, he spotted a marked Medicine Hat Police Service vehicle traveling in the opposite direction. He said, "Look at that! There's like 1500 cops in this City. There's something wrong with that!" By his estimate of the police to population ratio, Medicine Hat would have needed a census count of 1.2 million. At that time, MHPS had less than 120 sworn members.

He shook his head in disgust and muttered, "Bastards!". I replied, "Yep, they're all Bastards, every one!" When we arrived at my destination I grinned, and gave him a $5.00 tip on the fare.

14

Dispatch 9-1-1

Volvo

It was one of those boring, uneventful night shifts. The calls for service were few and far between and there were none in my patrol area. At those times, I tried to make work...self-generate... proactive policing.

I slowly cruised through the parking lot of an off-highway hotel, looking for anything of interest. A late model Volvo with out-of-province plates caught my eye. I radioed the licence plate number to dispatch.

One of our dispatchers queried the plate against the National computer system and reported no wants or warrants. She then gave me the registered owner information. "5-6...your plate comes back to a grey 1992 Vulva....". A moment to regain my composure then..."10-4 thank you".

The radio channel went silent for a few moments as members of my crew scoured hotel, motel and mall parking lots in search of Volvos to run their plates.

Water Dog

An emergency call came in and the Medicine Hat dispatcher, Sheree Perret answered, "9-1-1 Do you need Fire, Police or Ambulance?" The response she received was from a distraught female who was screaming into the phone, "MY DOG...OH MY GOD...MY DOG!" The screaming continued and the concerned dispatcher was finally able to determine the nature of the emergency. The woman, who resided in a County area outside of Medicine Hat, had discovered her missing dog floating in her basement cistern. She and her daughter had been drinking water drawn from that same cistern.

After determining that no one in the household was ill or in need of emergency medical attention, Sheree advised the caller that an employee from the Municipal District of Cypress would be sent out, but only during working hours the next day. The caller became enraged and subjected her to what she described as the worst profanity she had ever heard before the woman hung up.

Moments later the same woman called back, this time on a non-emergency line. When the answer was as before, she subjected Sheree to another tirade of cursing before hanging up. This attracted the attention of the on-duty Patrol Sergeant, who was known to be fussy when it came to protocol and a stickler for proper procedure. Upon being briefed about the caller, he gave Sheree detailed instructions as to how to she was to handle this person should she call back. Sure enough, she did call back and the Sergeant stood behind Ms. Perret, arms folded, waiting to see that his instructions were followed to the letter.

Sheree knew her job well enough, perhaps better than the Sergeant, so she decided to have some fun. As the caller was screaming across the phone line, Sheree surreptitiously hit the "mute" button for her headset. The caller could now hear nothing from the dispatcher's end of the line.

By this time, the Patrol Sergeant was demanding information. "Is she the same woman?" "Is she still insisting we attend?" "Is she still wanting us to get her dog?" With her headset still on mute, Sheree stood up from her chair and feigned anger and a total loss of patience as she yelled into the microphone, "YOU CRAZY WOMAN! I DON'T CARE IF YOU'VE BEEN DRINKING YOUR DOG ALL DARN NIGHT ... GET TO BED!" The Sergeant stood there, mouth hanging open and unable to utter a word.

Sheree then unmuted her headset and in a pleasant voice said, "Ma'am, I'm truly sorry to hear about what happened to your dog, but we just won't be able to send anyone tonight. I can send someone from the M.D. of Cypress over first thing in the morning." Resigned, the caller didn't scream or swear. She simply said, "That's it then, I'm going to kill myself." With this new threat of suicide, Sheree replied, "Ma'am, please stay on the line with me and we'll send someone right over."

I Just Want My Gun

Four dispatchers were on duty in the Medicine Hat 9-1-1- call centre on that summer evening. There was a full moon that night and they all knew from experience that odd or peculiar people often emerged when the Goddess Luna was at her largest. Although he had a history with the Medicine Hat Police Service, this was their first encounter with Joe. A call came through to the 9-1-1- console and was answered by Dispatcher Sheree Perret. "9-1-1, do you require Fire, Police or Ambulance?"

Joe replied slowly, "Hellllo...my name is Joe. I'm not going to hurt any...body. I'm not gonna' hurt...myself. I just want my gun." Joe told an agonizingly slow story about how he had been shooting gophers behind his trailer when two policemen showed up and took his gun away. Now Joe wanted his gun back. He sighed and said, "My name is Joe. I'm not going to hurt any...Body. I'm not gonna' hurt...Myself. I just want my gun." Sheree told Joe that the officers who could give him his gun back weren't working right then and that he should call back in the morning. Joe wished her a pleasant night and hung up.

About twenty minutes later a call came in on a non-emergency Police line. "My name is Joe. I'm not going to hurt any...Body. I'm not gonna' hurt...Myself. I JUST WANT MY GUN." The Police dispatcher told Joe to go to bed and not call again that night. Joe told her that she wasn't very nice and hung up.

Almost an hour passed when a call came in on a non-emergency Ambulance line. It was Joe again. "My name is Joe. I'm not going to hurt any...BODY. I'm not gonna' hurt...MYSELF. I JUST WANT MY GUN! Can you put it in the ambulance and bring it over to me in the trailer court?" Sheree had the dispatcher transfer the call back to her and said, "Joe, here's the deal. No one can get your gun for you tonight and I just want to warn you that if you keep calling us then we will have to send the police over to your place and they might arrest you. So, you see, I'm trying to help you out here Joe". Joe sighed and said that he was minding his own business, just sitting naked in his big chair in the living room and looking out at the moon. He said he just wanted his gun and he wasn't going to quit calling until someone brought it to him.

The police Patrol Sergeant and another officer found Joe at home, staring at the moon and as promised, naked and sitting in his big green vinyl recliner. As the Police officers radioed that they were on scene, Sheree could hear Joe in the background saying, "My name is Joe. I'm not going to hurt any...body. I'm not gonna' hurt...myself. I just want my gun." The next radio transmission was a out-of-breath call for backup. Joe was a large man, about six-foot-four and built like a bulldozer. It took four Police officers to arrest Joe.

I don't know if Joe ever went shooting gophers again with his toy gun.

Well Hello There

It was a warm weekend in July when Dispatcher Sheree Perret was working a night shift at the Medicine Hat 9-1-1 Emergency Fire console. The Dispatch Centre was busy, with plenty of complaints from the bars and of noisy backyard parties. The phone lines were lit up and the radios blared dispatches to Police, Fire and Ambulance units across the City.

A call came in reporting a basement fire in a home located in the Flats, what was then a run-down part of town. Sheree transmitted the location to the Fire Service as others dispatched Police to the scene and placed Ambulance on stand-by.

The Police contingent that night was led by a first-time "Acting Sergeant". Occasionally, when the Patrol Sergeant was away on leave or a training course, a Senior Constable would fill in as the on-street Supervisor for that shift. The Constable chosen for this duty had to first demonstrate his or her ability by prior satisfactory performance and had to have successfully written and passed the "Sergeant's Exam", a prerequisite for promotion.

When I was a Constable, I confided to another Member that I was intimidated by the prospect of writing the "Sergeant's Exam". He smirked and pointed in the direction of one particular Sergeant, saying, "He passed". Point taken and I passed too.

This Acting Sergeant was first-on-scene, and found smoke billowing out of the home. He parked his Supervisor's SUV in the alley directly behind the house and enthusiastically began to instruct his crew in the principles of crowd control and preservation of evidence.

When the Ladder Truck and Engine 3 from the Fire Department came flying up the alley with lights and siren, they were not pleased to find a police vehicle blocking their path. A terse message promptly came over the air, "Dispatch, advise your police to get that vehicle out of our way!" The Acting Sergeant was in his vehicle in a heartbeat and as he pulled away, he radioed, "Engine 3, alley clear for your units," before parking in a nearby backyard. All he got in reply was a curt, "10-4" and the fire crews went to work.

Suddenly, an unfamiliar voice came over the air, "Hellllo… anybody out there?" Sheree replied, "Who is this? Please identify." She heard a chuckle and a male voice asking, "So, how are things in the dispatch place tonight?" Moments later, he continued, "Well, it appears I'll have to leave soon." In the background of this broadcast Sheree heard, "Open this door!" and "Get out of the vehicle!". The guy made one final radio transmission, "Boy, this sure is fun being a policeman."

About fifteen minutes later a grim-faced Acting Sergeant led a young guy wearing handcuffs and a huge smile down the hallway of the police station. As they passed the Dispatch window the young man called out, "Hey ladies, that sure was fun. Thanks for making my night."

I'm quite sure that Constable never left his vehicle unlocked and unattended again.

15

Patrols

Stop, Or Else

The biker rolled into the parking lot of one of our off-highway clubs. He was full of himself and decided that this hick-town bar belonged to him.

He was a big man and it wasn't long before he started to assault patrons and staff, using his motorcycle helmet as a weapon. Of course, the cops were called.

I was probably the fifth or sixth unit to arrive, so his dance card was full and there was no room for anyone else to join in. I saw a large man flexing his biceps with policemen hanging off his arms. The guys were struggling to gain control of this monster. Finally, they took him to the ground. He still had lots of fight in him and our people were in danger of being seriously injured. One of our members decided to put a stop to it with a well-placed soccer kick to the biker's "little boy parts". That was the end of that...he groaned and said, "Okay I'm done".

After he was loaded into the prisoner transport van, I commented to the heavily breathing police members present. I said, "You guys have to work smarter, not harder".

I then walked over to the biker's custom built, no doubt $100K Harley Davidson motorcycle and pulled out my extendable baton. It made a sound like "Shhhlick" as I as I brought it out and posed menacingly over the bike.

I said, "I would have told him. Stop right there...or the bike gets it!!!".

Waste Not, Want Not

He was a very good Detective. His ability to ferret out bad guys, get confessions and obtain convictions gained him the respect of Prosecutors, Defence Council and most of the criminal element in Medicine Hat. But like us all, the Detective Sergeant started out as a young Patrol Constable and was often saddled with the humdrum jobs no one else wanted to do.

A poor fellow had come to the conclusion that it was time for lunch. He made himself a sandwich and then, in a moment of despair, he came to the conclusion that it was time to end it all. He was successful. The Constable was assigned the task of maintaining continuity of the premises until the Forensic Unit arrived to process the scene and collect all the evidence.

The Constable had missed breakfast that day and the job of watching over the scene was a long and boring task. No one had offered to relieve him and his husky body was demanding food. On the table was the very delicious looking uneaten sandwich made by the recently departed.

He concluded that the sandwich would not be entered into evidence and the deceased wasn't likely to object.

We Attack at Dawn

He was once a member of Canada's elite Commando-like military force, known only as JTF2. He retired briefly from the military to try his hand at civilian policing, but eventually decided that it was not his cup of tea and returned to the Army. The Constable and I were partnered up for a few days after he first joined our Police Service.

I recall one early summer morning when we were just getting ready to finish our nightshift. Police dispatch advised us that a female caller had reported prowlers in her yard. She said that there were strangers in her back yard and that they were drinking and burning wood in her fire-pit. The caller was terrified.

We arrived moments later. As we approached the house from the front. My partner silently hand-signaled that he would take the left flank to the rear of the property and I was to take the right. He was the military tactician but I understood a "classic pincer movement" when I saw one. We could hear voices from the enemy encampment and began our early dawn attack.

Now maybe it's because I was closer to fifty than I was to forty, but I barely got around the first corner when I heard the screams. Arriving a heartbeat later, I saw two males on the ground in obvious discomfort, while the Constable was in the process of easily disabling and downing the third suspect, a very drunk female.

All three were submitting painfully to his control when the caller opened the back door and said, "Oh my, those look like the people that moved in upstairs last week".

I said to the Constable, "Okay just ease up and let me do the talking, okay?" A short explanation was made and we all parted well, the drunks saying how "neat" it was to be put down that fast. In fact, they marveled at how tough we cops are.

We Just Want to Help Out

Peter and Paul were identical twins. They were in their mid-to-late fifties when I first met them at their shared home in an older area of Medicine Hat, Alberta. They were what some people referred to as "winos".

Their home wasn't the only thing they shared. When one of the brothers divorced his wife, she simply changed bedrooms and took up with the other. Once they told me that when one ran afoul of the law and was sentenced to serve an intermittent sentence, they would take turns serving the weekend jail time. They thought it was a great joke as no one could tell them apart.

Another man committed a break and enter to a nearby butcher shop, stealing two full, dressed pigs. Fearing that he would be caught with the stolen goods, he took the four sides of pork to Peter and Paul, asking that they hold onto them for him until the heat died down. They agreed and later told me, "We just wanted to help out".

I received confidential information about the location of the pinched pork. When I showed up at their house, I was cordially invited in by Peter and Paul. "Yes Officer, those pigs are here" and I was shown to an unheated back porch where they hung from the rafters.

Peter and Paul were so friendly and cooperative that I almost hated to charge them. I thanked them both for being so honest with me and their reply was, "We just want to help out". After issuing them each a Promise to Appear in Court to face a charge of Possession of Stolen Property, I called one of our Bylaw Enforcement trucks to the property to seize the meat.

It was the middle of a winter night and the back yard of the property was covered in snow. I asked Peter and Paul to carry the carcasses to the Bylaw truck and they happily complied. The two less-than-sober brothers then staggered through the snow carrying the full sides of pork. Peter stumbled and looked at Paul, or maybe Paul stumbled and looked at Peter, I don't know. Whichever, one said to the other, "If we're being charged, how come we're hauling these pigs?"

I said to the two brothers, "Because you just want to help out". They both grinned and finished loading the truck.

It Was Pink

This normally busy north-south thoroughfare was all but deserted at that time of the morning. I saw a driver approaching a traffic light that just turned from green to amber. He was a full quarter-block away, but rather than slowing to stop, he floored it. It wasn't even close. I pulled him over for running a red light.

Now given the time of day and the absence of traffic, I was prepared to just check his sobriety and issue a warning. He decided to earn a ticket. When I informed him that he had been stopped for running a red light he replied with a sneer, "It wasn't red...it was PINK!"

I then asked him to produce his driver's licence, along with the vehicle registration and insurance documents. He said, "Do you know who I am?" I didn't, but he puffed out his chest and informed me that he was the owner of a popular one-of-a-kind fast food restaurant in the City. I told him that he was getting a traffic ticket. Thinking back, I probably should have asked him if he wanted fries with that.

"Well, I'm a personal friend of Inspector (so-and-so) and I'll be telling him about this!" I said, "Go ahead, he's retired now and I never liked that SOB anyway".

The Turnip Truck

Late one cold winter night, two MHPS Constables surprised two young men outside of the Royal Hotel bar in Medicine Hat. The two men had slipped outside for a short "toke" of their favorite cigarette.

As the Constables approached, they could smell the heavy pungent odor of marihuana in the air, but having been alerted, the men had just enough time to dispose of the evidence. One of the Constables looked at the two jacketless men shivering in the cold. The temperature was so low that they were vibrating. He said, "What are you two doing out here?" One man blurted out, "We just came out to cool off", and resumed his shivering. The Constable looked at him sternly and said, "Do you think I just fell off a turnip truck? Do you see a turnip truck around here?"

The man silently pointed to the ground. There, believe it or not, was a large turnip, frozen into the icy ground. The Constable paused a moment, and he and his partner broke into laughter. God must have been rewarding those two young men that night for some good deed they had done. The Constable looked at them and commanded, "Get the hell out of here".

These Boots Aren't Made for Walkin'

He had the best-looking boots in the Department.

These days, Policemen tend to wear boots constructed of Gore-Tex and other man-made materials that are designed to be durable, comfortable and weatherproof. These materials are not designed to receive the high level of "spit polish" the old-style leather Police boots were given.

In those days, we all showed up for duty with boots that were clean and shiny, befitting an organization that was steeped with old-school military tradition. Some guys just excelled at it. This Constable's boots were so shiny, you could shave in the reflection from the toecaps.

During his days off, a very mischievous person somehow got into a locker that was not his own and took a pair of boots that did not belong to him. The slender, fine blade of a coping saw was applied to each boot, just behind the toecaps. The saw slid past the uppers and all the way through the soles. Once each toe was effectively severed, they were replaced, being held in place by some glue. A touch of shoe polish on the seam completed the effect.

The Constable returned to work, donned his uniform, and only made a few steps before the toes of his boots fell off. Fortunately, most Policemen kept at least two pair of boots in their locker.

He Didn't Know the Gun Was Loaded

A call came in about a B&E in Progress. Bad guys had busted into someone's house and a witness called to report it. We raced to the scene and surrounded the premises. Entry was made by one of our K-9 officers, his dog, and a Patrol member acting as cover. The rest of us waited outside and secured the perimeter.

The Staff Sergeant stood nearby me as we waited for the search of the residence to be completed. I decided to have some fun. I told the Staff Sergeant, "I haven't carried live ammo since '83". He looked at me with wide eyes, and said "WHAT?" "Yeah", I said, "It's too scary out here...I don't want to be shot with my own gun." He bought it and said, "Now Dave, that's dangerous... you have to have a loaded gun." "Oh No", I countered, "I have full magazines on my belt...if I need them, I'll use them, but I won't carry live ammo in my gun." After a pause I said, "It's just safer that way."

The Staff Sergeant was beside himself. He didn't know what to say. He had never encountered a Policeman with an empty gun before. His arguments for carrying "locked and loaded" were becoming more intense. He was genuinely worried for my safety. I let it go on for a bit before I confessed that I was "JUST KIDDING".

Sorry

Some people love to complain about the Police. They even try to make it a spectator sport, especially during the summer months when it's hot and there's no hockey on TV.

I had an earlier telephone conversation with a woman whom I warned that should she continue interfering with another family, she could face legal consequences. This woman promptly telephoned the duty Staff Sergeant complain about how I had treated her. She ranted loudly into the phone for about ten minutes. He couldn't get a word in edge-wise. After he hung up, my Staff Sergeant told me, "I see why you had such a problem with her, she's a...."

Unsatisfied, the woman showed up at the Police station later that evening to speak to the Staff Sergeant personally. She demanded some satisfaction. I was seated at a nearby desk doing paperwork, but because we had only spoken to each other over the telephone, she didn't know who I was. I watched as she went into the Staff Sergeant's office, accompanied by two friends and her little lap dog. Again, she began to rant and rave. Her female friend stood there, silently cheering her on. The guy looked very uncomfortable, obviously wishing it was hockey season. I think the dog wanted to pee. She went up one side of my Staff Sergeant and down the other, complaining about how I didn't treat her right. He tried his darndest to calm her down but she wouldn't listen to reason.

Enough's enough. I wasn't going to sit there and let Staff take that abuse alone, especially since the problem was "apparently" my fault. I walked into the office and identified myself to the woman. Before she could say another word, I said, "MA'AM, I AM VERY SORRY that you misunderstood what I told you". She looked at me with her mouth open, her next verbal barrage now stuck in her throat. After a moment she said, "Well, as long as you're apologizing, then I'm satisfied". She left a happy woman.

After the woman left, Staff looked at me with a grin and said, "You're sorry that SHE misunderstood?"

You Missed a Piece

I watched a "training video" in briefing. A State Trooper somewhere in the U.S.A. had encountered a total lunatic during a traffic stop. That Trooper kept his cool and, in so doing, produced one of the funniest "police dashcam" videos I have ever seen.

About two weeks later, I was working radar in a residential playground zone. It was a sunny, summer weekend afternoon and there were people everywhere. Young mothers were in the park watching their children play and across the street, neighborhood men were giving their lawns a fresh mowing.

The alarm on my radar was set for a touch over playground zone and this guy blew though at more than twenty over. I waved over the speeder, obtained his particulars, and returned to my car to write the ticket. When I presented the offender with his Violation Ticket, he saw the amount of the fine and went ballistic. The whole neighborhood stopped to see what I was going to do with the crazy man that erupted from the once speeding car. The guy came flying out of his car and began to jump up and down as he screamed, "Are you out of your fucking mind!!"

I thought, "Hmmm...I've seen a video just like this" and held my ground. As the irate man ranted and raved, I stood there silently, hands clasped loosely together over my belt buckle, slowly rocking back and forth on the heels of my boots. My lack of reaction enraged the driver and he furiously threw his wallet to the ground. His credit cards, money, and personal papers were strewn across the road.

I was conscious of the neighbors watching me. They waited in anticipation to see what was going to happen next. I looked at the man, and then pointed to the ground where his wallet lay. I said, "You'd better pick that up or I'm going to have to give you a ticket for littering". He went berserk, screaming in a high-pitched voice, but he complied, scrambling to retrieve his wallet and contents. As he was picking up the pieces, he called me every dirty name he could think of. I thought again of the State Trooper in the video and remained calm. When he overlooked a scrap of paper, I mimicked the Trooper in the video and said, "You missed a piece".

This guy was beat and he knew it. The whole neighborhood actually applauded as he finally, and slowly, drove away. Many thanks to that State Trooper who inspired my response.

The Policeman is Your Friend

Little kids love the Police. We have uniforms, and guns, and handcuffs, and big rings of keys. We have radios and whistles and flashlights on our belts. Our cars have loud sirens and all sorts of flashing lights. Parents and teachers often tell the little ones, "The Policeman is your friend".

So, it came as no surprise one afternoon when I saw a very excited little boy of maybe four or five years running from his house to the sidewalk along the street. I slowed my car so he could get a good look and prepared to wave at him.

He reached the sidewalk and gave me his greeting, an extended middle finger, as he yelled, "Fuckin' PIG!!!"

I was stunned and almost stopped. Then I thought, "Who taught him this?" I asked myself if such people would respond positively to my concern. I concluded that they would not and possibly might punish the child for drawing attention to their residence. So, not knowing what to do, I drove away.

This Town Ain't Big Enough for the Two of Us

The Sergeant was born one hundred years too late.

So here we were in the late 1990's. Fed up with the antics of a transient criminal, Sarge went face to face with the man. With his nose barely an inch from the bad guy's, he said in a low and ominous voice that harbored a serious threat, "I'm giving you until sundown to get out of town". And he meant it.

Unlawfully at Large

Many parents have received similar calls at all hours of the day or night. One of their children has fallen astray and run afoul of the law. Then it's "Mom or Dad, please help me".

Constable Andy McGrogan, who later became the Chief of Police in Medicine Hat, was then one of our K-9 Officers. He was on a day off when the call came from an animal control officer who had captured Andy's Police Service Dog Tracer running at large. But I can imagine the call had Tracer himself been able to speak.

"Hello, Andy? This is Tracer.... I must have left my licence on my other collar...can you bail me out.... PUHLEEEEZE!" This incident was later immortalized in a City of Medicine Hat Animal Control cartoon poster reminding pet owners to licence their animals.

It Wasn't Me

If they were only all this easy.

He drove a real piece of garbage car. It was old. It was rusty. There wasn't a square inch of the vehicle that wasn't scratched, scraped or dented. Of course, he denied being responsible for the hit and run motor vehicle accident I was investigating.

"Well Sir, could you please explain how your licence plate came to be imbedded in the back of that parked car?"

Crack-Up

"Good police work" tends to be a recipe of ingredients that very often includes being in the right place at the right time, a pinch of luck, and, most important, a sizeable measure of paying attention to what you see and hear. And so, for the second time in as many months, members of our Patrol Teams arrested suspects for homicides from a major Canadian city.

In the first case, our Patrolman stopped a suspect just because he drove by the area "too many times" late at night. The suspect came out of his car with a knife...our man raised the ante by drawing his gun. The suspect obviously remembered that old adage, "It's stupid to bring a knife to a gunfight" and surrendered. He spontaneously announced that the car he was driving was stolen. The Constable must have replied something like "Okay, you're under arrest". At that point the suspect said, "You may as well arrest me for murder too" and confessed to killing the car's owner and committing an unrelated armed robbery.

In the second case the newspaper reported that members of the Medicine Hat Police Service had arrested the murder suspect after a "routine traffic stop". Let me assure you that there is nothing routine about a traffic stop that involves the suspect fleeing the Police at high speed, while at the same time smoking a crack pipe, inserting an "eight-ball" of crack cocaine into a bodily orifice, and ultimately causing his vehicle to roll over.

Field Sobriety Test

One of my favorite field sobriety tests from long ago was a simple question, "Is Mickey Mouse a dog or a cat?"

The Strongest Man in the World

We were parked side-by-side and I was visiting with an R.C.M.P. member. The Constable was of French Canadian decent. He casually reached for the radio microphone to relay a message to another unit. Then he then began to chuckle. Seeing my confusion, he told me a story, a memory flash-back from long ago.

It went back to his first days of training as an Auxiliary Constable when he had been partnered up with a senior Regular Member Constable. Throughout the day he observed the senior member make and receive radio calls as they went about their duties. Eventually, the senior member instructed him to make a radio call.

Try as he might, the new Constable could not free the microphone from its dash bracket.

The senior member finally had to demonstrate that one lifted the microphone from the clip that held it securely to the dash. The new Constable thought the circular disk on the back of the mike was a magnet, and that it pulled straight away from it's mount.

In heavily French accented English, the member laughed at himself as he told me, "I said to 'im, tank Christ! I 'tought you were da strongest man in da world".

Davey Boy to the Sin Bin

"Whatch you mean rasslin' ain't real?"

David "Davey Boy" Smith, otherwise known as "The British Bulldog," was a star of Calgary's Stampede Wrestling and later the WWF. He was also regarded as a super-hero in the U.K. wrestling arenas. In the early 90's, he had a night in the ring at the Medicine Hat Arena.

My partner for the night was Rick Wigle. We were both on days off but volunteered for the "pay-duty", which was extra overtime cash paid for by the event, not by taxpayers. Rick and I were posted at the wrestler's entrance, to keep curious fans from getting to the change rooms.

During the bouts, several of the wrestlers visited briefly and watched the matches with us. One approached from behind and good-naturedly slapped another across the shoulders. He grinned and said to me, "I've got to wrestle this prick next...can you give him a shot of pepper spray?"

"The British Bulldog" was carded to fight "Kamala". Although he was a huge black man born in the southern U.S.A., Kamala was billed as the "Ugandan Headhunter". He appeared at ring side wearing a loin cloth, war paint and carrying a spear. Kamala's "Manager" wore his signature Safari suit and a tropical pith helmet.

Later that evening, Rick and I had a casual discussion with the event Manager who stopped by our post. We learned that Kamala was planned to defeat The British Bulldog at this event.

We both fell silent. We then quickly explained to the event Manager that a good portion of the fans in the stands were British soldiers who had shown up specifically to watch Smith. In fact, the nearby U.K. Army base had purchased five or six hundred tickets for their members, many of whom had shown up under the influence. We stressed that our small contingent could not guarantee the safety of their performers if it went bad for the fan's favorite.

I don't think he took us seriously until mid-bout, when a group of five or six British soldiers pressed forward toward the ring, bearing a stout pole with a spear point, from which the Union Jack hung proudly. They were intercepted by ring security before anyone was impaled. A last-minute change of plan and The British Bulldog won the match!

At the end of the evening, the wrestlers were ushered out a back door to their waiting vehicles. An excited mob of cheering British soldiers began a chant from behind the barricades as Smith approached. Despite being British himself, Smith couldn't understand them. He turned to Rick and I and said, "What are they saying?" Rick grinned and said, "Davey Boy to the Sin Bin... Davey Boy to the Sin Bin". Smith said, "Sin Bin?" We explained that the local Assiniboia Hotel tavern, the "Sin Bin", was the quasi-official watering hole for the British Forces in Medicine Hat and that he was receiving an invitation to join his fans there. Smith chuckled and said that sounded like great fun. Rick hopped in the car with Smith and navigated to the bar.

And so, "The British Bulldog" partied with Her Majesty's troops at the "Sin Bin" and I'd reckon he didn't pay for a drink all night.

Mutual of Omaha

He was actually a nice guy once you got to know him. His acts of charity within and well beyond the community proved that. But this particular Staff Sergeant was generally regarded as a bully on the job. He preyed upon any of his crew whom he considered to be weak.

I recall one dayshift where Staff called Constable Dellrae Sharpe on the radio. He said, "Sharpe! My office! Now!"

Dellrae was working Patrol Area 7, which was then the neighboring Town of Redcliff. "Yes Staff!" and as she drove into the City her mind was spinning, wondering what was wrong. His tone of voice foreshadowed a serious problem. It was a long drive to the station and once there, Dellrae nervously presented herself at the Staff Sergeant's office.

Meekly she asked, "Is there something wrong Staff?" His reply was, "Nope, I just realized that you and I haven't gone for coffee together yet".

I often compared this Staff Sergeant to a lion on the Mutual of Omaha TV series "Wild Kingdom". He would lurk in the grass and stare at the herd of Zebra before him. Once he selected one, the others could bounce in front of him, crossing their eyes and sticking out their tongues. He was focused on his prey and no other. Of course, once he had his fun, he moved on to a new Zebra.

When it was my turn, I got the familiar radio call. "Peskor! My office! Now!" As I stood in front of his desk he leaned forward and said, "Do you have a problem with me?" I leaned across my side of his desk and said, "Nope. Do you have a problem with me?" He said "No" and we went for coffee.

Years later I was the Sergeant in charge of the Criminal Intelligence Unit. I had arrived at work early that day and wandered through the Patrol area near shift change. I saw a few nightshift Constables finishing up their paperwork, with Staff hovering over them like a dark cloud.

As our eyes met, I yelled out, "Hey Staff, when are you going to fucking retire and let someone else have your job?"

Those Constables were gobsmacked! I'm sure they were ready to duck under their desks to avoid the confrontation that was sure to follow.

The Staff Sergeant looked at me with a grin and said, "When I'm ready, you'll be the first to know". He didn't keep that promise...I was the second to know!

Who Let the Cat Out of the Box?

One of the all time classic practical jokes from days long gone by. First you have to capture an alley cat. Then you stuff it into the glove box of another Policeman's car. Close the lid carefully. Now I have to say that no animals were hurt during this stunt. Some Policemen may have been, but again, no animals were hurt.

As the glove box was carefully closed, the cat would soon calm down and relax in the dark quiet place. At least until the victim returned and started the car. The noise and vibration invariably caused the feline stowaway to stir and cause a fuss. Hearing scratching from inside the glove box, the natural reaction was to open it up.

Alley cats confined in Police car glove boxes reach maximum velocity in less than a second. They also hiss and spit and scratch.

Bombs Away!

Back when it was routine to have the most junior members "walk the beat", they often became targets of the more senior members who were assigned to cars. Every rookie delegated to walk a beat was responsible for his specific zone and Saint Michael, Patron Saint of Police Officers, protect him if there was an undetected break and enter in his area during his tour of duty. They walked up and down their beat in all weather, conscious of the invisible surveillance of their Patrol Sergeant.

Alleys are generally very dark, very deserted, and very quiet. As one Rookie walked the alley, shaking hands with every doorknob along the way, mischievous persons lay in wait. Armed with spent fluorescent tubes retrieved from local office dumpsters, pranksters waited in ambush at the top level of a nearby car parkade as the beat man approached below.

"Bombs away!" Fluorescent tubes, when dropped from a great height and in the dead of night, upon striking a solid surface such as an alleyway, make a loud noise reminiscent of gunfire. It was a great way to get someone's heart started in the dark hours of the morning.

Bad Actors

We had enough of these guys. The two men blew into town and had been committing sophisticated break and enters without fear. They used Police scanners to warn them of any Police activity in their area of operation and headset two-way radios to communicate with each other. They cut holes into store ceilings and rappelled down ropes like New York City cat burglars. We knew who they were and formed a rapid response plan.

An alarm came in, and by bad luck, we missed the two bad guys by minutes. But we knew where they lived and surrounded the Motel where our two suspects were staying. We really didn't have sufficient legal grounds to make an entry. Aware of their use of Police scanner radios, we scripted the following text, recited in stilted speech like a bunch of bad actors.

"Uhh-Gee-Whiz...it-sure-is-cold-out-here".

"Uhh-yeah-it-sure-is. I-hope-that-those-guys-get-back-with-the-Search-Warrant-soon. We-don't-have-enough-guys-to-cover-the-back-of-this-Motel."

"Yeah, if-they-came-out-the-back-right-now-we-couldn't-catch-them."

Just then, the door burst open. Two men ran from the scene. One ran right into the arms of waiting Police members. The second man ran towards the nearby #3 Highway. He had a good lead.

One of our Constables stood about 6′ 00″ tall and weighed next to nothing, but he ran like a deer. He spotted bad guy number two and his radar locked in. I saw him pursuing the second suspect through the snow. Fifty yards.... jettison the winter coat.

Forty yards.... need...more...speed... pitch the radio.

Thirty yards...must...go...faster...dump the flashlight.

Twenty yards...eject assorted and sundry items.

Impact! Our Constable hit the bad guy in a "poof" of powdered snow. Ill-gotten coins and paper money exploded into the air.

You know, those-darn-guys-never-did-get-there-with-that-search-warrant.

Do You See Anyone You Know?

As cops, we possess a wide variety of utensils in our investigative tool belts. We have fingerprints, DNA, ballistics, hair and fibre evidence, and witness statements to name a few.

Back in the day, one of those tools was the lineup. I once witnessed what was likely to be one of the last real-person lineups conducted by my Police Service. At the time, pursuant to the *Identification of Criminals Act*, we had the lawful authority to scour the streets in search of persons who resembled the suspect and compel (kidnap) them to accompany us to the Police Station where they were placed into a "lineup" with our suspect. Just like on TV, a rack of blinding lights prevented them from seeing the victim or witness who viewed the event from behind a one-way glass window.

The participants turned in unison to the commands, "Face left", Face Front", "Face Right". I wanted to command, "Put your left foot in, put your left foot out, put your left foot in and you shake it all about", however the "Hokey Pokey" and any other shenanigans were strictly forbidden. For obvious civil rights reasons this practice was later abandoned. The "live" lineup was replaced with the "photo lineup".

A photo lineup is an array of police booking photos including the suspect and about five other persons who share similar facial characteristics. The witness is simply asked if he or she sees anyone who is familiar to them.

In the early morning hours, the victim suffered a very severe assault in an alley near her home. The suspect was a new acquaintance from the bar. A Constable was assigned to guard the area and any evidence within until the Forensic Identification Unit arrived to process the crime scene by light of day. As dawn broke, the Constable was shocked to witness a crow swoop into the scene and make off with the victim's dentures. This was clearly a case of obstruction of justice and evidence tampering.

In an effort to identify the culprit, the Forensic Identification Unit quickly assembled a photo line up for our witness, the Constable. He was presented with a photo lineup consisting of a pigeon, a robin, a crow, a magpie, a sparrow and a chicken.

Made You Look

Everyone, both cops or crooks, liked Constable Dan Cornet. He was quick of wit and always ready to deliver a joke or a groaner pun. You were rarely bored during a shift with Danny.

Like the time he wanted to form the "Redcliff Police Domestic Intervention Unit". He thought we could "Doo Wop" dance into the scene of a family dispute with a 1950's "Shovel Step" or "Choir Step", all the while singing the Righteous Brothers song, "You lost that lovin' feelin".

Before joining the Redcliff Town Police Department, Danny was a Special Constable with the Royal Canadian Mounted Police. As such, he was not a fully sworn member of the R.C.M.P. and performed prisoner transport and other duties that would free up Regular members from such mundane tasks.

Back then, the Medicine Hat detachment of the Royal Canadian Mounted Police was located in a tiny building near the Medicine Hat Hospital. A "high-rise" apartment building stood across the back alley. In the summertime, a female resident of this building was fond of sunbathing on her balcony. She wore the skimpiest of bathing suits, presumably to minimize tan lines. Danny was fond of performing "surveillance" on that particular balcony with a pair of binoculars from a back room. Before Danny showed up for his scheduled shift, someone pressed the eyepieces of those binoculars onto a rubber-stamp inkpad.

The detachment members were going for a pre-shift coffee and called Danny to join them. When he emerged from the back room, they saw what appeared to be a chubby raccoon standing before them. Danny had thick black ink stains circling his eyes.

They could have let him go out in public like that but they didn't. After much laughter, Danny was told to look in the mirror. He said it took him considerable time, and a significant amount of bathroom cleanser to remove those marks of shame.

Rules of Engagement

Did you ever get called onto the carpet for doing your job?

I was a "working Sergeant" in the small eight-man Redcliff Police Department. That meant that I was not only a Supervisor but was also expected to take and investigate complaints. Our members did that, despite their rank.

Your next call could be a parking complaint or a robbery or a homicide. If you caught the call, it was your file. Of course, you could always expect support and advice from more experienced members if you needed it. From top to bottom, we gained a lot of experience and our files were generally well received by the Crown Prosecutor's office.

In the early 90's, our small Police Department was absorbed into the much larger Medicine Hat Police Service when the City contracted policing services to the Town. I was now once again a Constable and wore a different patch on the shoulders of my shirt. My patrol car had a different decal on the doors, and we dealt with different people on different streets. However, our new Police Service neglected to fully explain the rules of engagement when they cut us loose.

I was dispatched to a break and enter at a small grocery store and spoke to the proprietor. I surveyed the scene, requested Ident for pictures and prints, took a statement, offered some advice on securing the premises and assured the owner the I would canvas the neighborhood in an attempt to locate a witness. Being a first-generation immigrant, he was impressed by the competence of Canadian police. Having completed my investigation, I turned to leave when he said, "Wait! I have bad cheque!"

So, I started a second non-sufficient-funds (NSF) cheque investigation. That involved a second statement and a trip to the Bank where the cheque was drawn against to obtain the account information that was, at that time, available to law enforcement without warrant. Report submitted...coffee time.

My Staff Sergeant's voice blared over the radio, "Peskor! My office! Now!!" That tone did not bode well. No doubt other crew members who coveted the location of my locker were calling "dibs". I entered the Staff Sergeant's office where he sat, leaning back in his chair with a scowl on his face. He tossed a file across his desk in my direction and said, "What is this?' I saw that it was my NSF cheque case. I was immediately confused.

Was the witness statement sub-standard? Had I failed to collect sufficient banking information? Did I not make a compelling nexus between the business, property, bank account and the accused? I had done hundreds of these investigations before and had no idea what was wrong. The Staff Sergeant eventually conceded that the case file was, in his words, "adequate".

I will never forget what he said next. He growled, "We pay Detectives to do this". And that was the last fraud related file I ever investigated.

Black and Tan

Constable Sean Boser was, to my knowledge, Medicine Hat's first black Policeman. He has since moved on to a stellar career with the R.C.M.P.

Sean and I were partnered together for an evening when he first joined the Medicine Hat Police Service. That night we were working the north side area 5 when a report of a car prowling in progress came in. The caller described two males who were at that very moment breaking into her neighbor's car. Sean and I sped to the scene and as we rounded the corner our headlights illuminated the bad guys. One ran west and the other ran north. The first suspect presented the best opportunity for capture so Sean and I both took after him. Our K-9 unit was not far away and we directed him after the second suspect. Sean quickly ran down our suspect and I arrived breathlessly moments later, just in time to assist with the handcuffing.

As we escorted our prisoner back to our car, we met up with Tim Schottner, our K-9 officer. He told us that the second suspect must have jumped into a nearby getaway car because the scent track stopped abruptly. He tugged on his German Shepherd's leash and laughed, saying, "What's black and tan and looks good on a car prowler?" I proudly threw my arm around my partner's shoulder and said, "What's black and white and looks good on a car prowler?"

What the Five Fingers Said to the Face

Alberta in the early 1970's was in the midst of an oil boom. Events in the Middle East caused world oil prices to skyrocket overnight and Alberta was awash in the stuff. Thousands of people flooded into the Province to ride the winning pony and, hopefully, get rich quick. Oil patch workers made fantastic wages. They worked hard and they played even harder. Some of their favorite playgrounds were the bars.

He wasn't a huge man, nor was he small. Although obviously fit, the Constable was of average height, weight and build. But everyone was amazed at his handiness in a bar fight. He would wade into the frequent bar room scrimmages, swatting at combatants who continued fighting after the arrival of the

Police. One or two smacks from him and they went down, and all with an open hand!

The secret of his prowess was finally revealed. Prior to entering one barfight, another Calgary Police Service member observed the Constable surreptitiously slip a pair of steel handcuffs into the palm of his gloved right hand.

You Hairball!

Medicine Hat Police Service uniformed patrol crews work twelve-hour shifts. Each shift is preceded by a "Briefing", attended by all oncoming patrol members, traffic members and a representative from dispatch. Sometimes members from Major Crimes or the Drug Unit were present. Once in a while, a "White Shirt" would show up.

These briefings were presided over by the Patrol Sergeant who brought us up to speed on complaints and arrests from the previous shift. He also informed us about warrants for wanted persons and BOLOs (Be-On-The-Lookout-For) for persons and vehicles of interest. Complaints from, and requests for special attention to, this area or that rounded out the session.

Occasionally, I succumbed to the urge to lighten things up. We were all transferred to different crews from time to time, depending on our expertise or experience and the needs of the Service. One of my favorite crews was overseen by a particular Sergeant, known for his no-nonsense and by the book manner. Although he would never admit it, he did have a sense of humour, although it was well camouflaged under layers of spit and polish. For some reason, he allowed me to get away with my antics with only a token scolding.

I once rigged his chair adjustment lever in the briefing room. When he sat down, I stood at attention, saluted and loudly hummed "Taps" as he slowly sunk to nose level at the front desk.

On another occasion, the Sergeant had just started briefing when I rose from my chair and grabbed the back of my neck, complaining loudly about pain from a locked-up vertebra. No one knew that I had concealed one of those clear, hard plastic drink cups under my jacket in my armpit. As I grimaced and howled in mock pain, I rapidly twisted my neck at the same time as I crushed the cup between my arm and my chest. It made a terrifying crunch sound and everyone in the room, including the Sergeant, was stunned. I sighed loudly and said, "Oh...that feels better". Sarge was concerned and asked if I was okay. I said "sure" and removed the broken cup from my jacket. "Peskor...you hairball!!

Oh, and then there was the time in Briefing, when I presented Sarge with a genuine, handcrafted, alien-resistant tin foil helmet.

The Rubber Cheque

Back in the days before debit cards, people actually hand-wrote personal cheques. Everyone had a cheque book and every business accepted those pieces of paper as a promise of payment.

The guy I charged didn't write a "rubber cheque" in anticipation of his hard-earned paycheque which, through no fault of his own, arrived late leaving his bank account with insufficient funds. This man's cheque "bounced" because he wrote it against a bank account that had long been closed. He knew what he did and had no defence. Nevertheless, to stall his inevitable conviction and probable incarceration, he pled "Not Guilty".

On the day of the trial, I spoke briefly to the accused's lawyer outside the courtroom. The lawyer was confident that he had a defence that would, despite the nonexistence of a valid bank account, spare his client from jail. Knowing the accused's past history of defaulting on his debts I simply asked the lawyer, "Did he pay you?" He smiled and said, "Yes" as he produced a paid-in-full cheque for the cost of his representation. I looked at that cheque and then produced my exhibit, a cheque drawn against the exact same bank account and boldly stamped in red, "Account Closed".

When the case was called, the defence lawyer rose and addressed the Court, "Your Honour, my client changes his plea to guilty."

Better Late Than Never

After years of working for the eight-member Town of Redcliff Police Department, my colleagues and I were assimilated into the much larger, neighboring City of Medicine Hat Police Service. As small-town cops, we weren't used to having immediate backup. We just did our best with what we had at the time.

New to the Service, I was working a night shift when a call came in for police assistance at the Medicine Hat Moose Lodge parking lot. I arrived on scene and was met by our complainant, a gentleman I appraised to be in his late-seventies. His dates for the night were two lovely ladies, both of whom I reckoned were just a few years younger than he. They had no doubt enjoyed a nice dinner followed by an evening of entertainment, possibly by one of those local family bands that belted out old-time country music tunes at that club.

The night was young, but not these three, so they left to the parking lot where the gentleman's pickup truck was located. There they found the truck, with an unexpected stowaway on board. A young twenties-something man was passed out drunk in the cargo bed of the truck. Their efforts to wake him were unsuccessful. That was probably a good thing.

I dropped the tailgate for easier extraction and gave the man's boot a shake. He did not respond. I gave his boot another shake, this time more forcefully. All I received in response was a murmur. Too drunk to get out on his own, I decided to help him. So, I grabbed both ankles and started to yard him out of the truck bed. I moved the young man maybe six inches when he bolted upright and stared at me. Before I could say a word, the fight was on. He lunged from the truck box and began to throw punches at my face. I was in my early forties and this young man was half my age and twice my size. We went to the ground and I recall one of the old girls said, "Oh my!"

As we scrambled about, I knew I wasn't capable of taking this young man out...yet. To hell with all those fancy "police restraining techniques" we had been taught since joining the ranks of our new Service...I fell back on what I knew would work for me. So, I choked him out. The fingers of my right hand formed claws that constricted his windpipe and brought about an almost immediate submission. I managed to handcuff the big boy and somehow, stuffed him into the prisoner compartment of my patrol car.

I got behind the wheel of my PC and breathlessly spoke into the radio, using police ten codes to communicate that I was enroute to the police station and that I had a prisoner. I then said, "5-6 Dispatch...I'm gonna' need some...help...at cells...I don't think I...can go another...two minutes...with this guy." Several

Constables immediately announced that they were on their way to help at the lockup. One other Member chided me and said, "Dave...around here we usually call for backup BEFORE the fight is over."

Knotty Knickers

In the early 1990's, the Medicine Hat Police Service Headquarters building had an internal paging system. Pager units were placed throughout the building, from which you could enter a code into the keypad and communicate directly with a specific office or work area. Once your communication was completed, you pushed a button to close the line. You could also enter a code to broadcast your message over the building-wide speaker system. This was valuable when someone came to the Reception Counter to speak with a specific officer who was not presently in his or her work area, or when a Senior NCO was trying to locate a junior Constable who had been evading their inevitable counselling session.

One afternoon, a civilian female member working in the reception area made a building-wide "All Call" to notify an officer to report to the front counter. She forgot to close the line after she made the page.

Now when you used this system, the building speakers in your immediate area were automatically disabled to prevent the screech of audio feedback. Without noticing the bright red "on-line" indicator light on the pager unit, she would not have known her next words were to be broadcast to the entire MHPS universe.

Another female employee approached her desk and the two engaged in conversation. Our gal began to complain about the "wedgy" she was experiencing. She went on to describe, in great detail, just how her panties were uncomfortably bunching up in her "lady parts". Her knickers were definitely in a knot!

Every desk phone in the Reception area began ringing off the hook as other staff members tried to advise her to close the pager line.

16

Cigarettes

I'm Trying to Quit

So, I have a vice...I smoke cigarettes.

I took a prisoner to the Medicine Hat Hospital Emergency room to be checked out prior to his well-deserved incarceration. The Doctor, recent to Medicine Hat from South Africa, stitched him up and left a pair of nurses to clean up his other assorted scrapes under the watchful eye of another Medicine Hat Police Service member.

I was outside the room at the Nursing counter when the Doctor approached. He informed me that our prisoner would soon be fit for a night in jail.

As we spoke, he looked me up and down, no doubt comparing my uniform to that worn by the police in South Africa. He looked at the red stripe on my pant legs, my black leather basket weave stamped Sam Browne belt loaded with a radio, pepper spray, expandable baton and a brushed stainless steel semi-automatic pistol. Then he focused on my shirt-front where my name tag was pinned on one side and my medal ribbon bar was pinned to the other. Both chest pockets held square contents, one being my notebook, the other, my pack of smokes.

The Doctor looked me in the eye and said "So, you smoke?". Preparing myself for the inevitable lecture I said, "Yes, but I'm trying to quit". "Me too," he said, as he pulled out his pack. "Let's go outside. It's been a busy night and I'm dying for a smoke!".

Those Things Will Kill You

I stepped outside the front doors of the police station with Aaron Sheard, the civilian Manager of our Information Technology (IT) department. We planned on enjoying a smoke break. By this time, I had retired, turned in my gun and badge, and was employed under contract as a civilian Police Intelligence Analyst for the Organized Crime Unit of the Medicine Hat Police Service.

Just as we lit up, a sworn member passed by. Darren Lole was a burly plain clothes Constable on his second career after completing service as a high-ranking Non-Commissioned Officer in the British Army. His previous career marked him with an intimidating presence to those who didn't know him. I did however, know him, worked along side him, and found him to be a likeable man, even if he came across as overbearing and maybe scary to some.

As he passed us, Darren sneered and commented, "Those things will kill you". Aaron's eyes went wide and his jaw dropped when I replied, "Oh shut up!!" He must have expected that he was about to witness a terrible confrontation. Darren glared at us for a moment, then grinned and went on his way.

The Bodyguard

I attended a week long training course held at a venue in downtown Vancouver, B.C. It was an opportunity for my wife Margot and I to have a getaway together. The plan was that I would attend classes and she would explore and shop by day. We would have the evenings together.

Restaurant food can be a bit much for me after a few days on the road and we both like to stock up the Hotel room mini-fridge with fresh fruit, vegetables, deli meats and cheese when we travel. Add a nice bottle of wine and we can snack on what we want when we want.

After checking into our room at a somewhat upscale hotel chain, we approached a front desk clerk and I asked if there was a grocery store within walking distance. She gave us a look that said, "why on earth do you need a grocery store?" before telling us with a degree of certainty that there was no such business in that part of the city's downtown core. Resigned to making a cab trip to the outskirts the next day, we went outside to have a cigarette.

It was the early evening and, as is the case in most large urban centres, the demographics of those on the street began to change as the sun went down. It wasn't long before we were approached by one of the city's street people. He held out his hand, clutching two twenty-five cent coins in his fingers.

He said, "Can I buy a smoke from you?" I said, "No, you can't buy a smoke from us, but you can have one". I gave him a cigarette, and as he lit up, I asked him if there was a grocery store nearby. He happily gave us directions to a small shop just around the corner. We followed his route and found it, right where he said it would be.

The next day, while I attended classes, my wife explored and did some shopping as planned. She told me that she gave the same man a few more smokes and, in exchange, he became her unofficial bodyguard, keeping other street people from bothering her.

My Smoking Buddy

I think that I may be the only Policeman to ever testify under oath about his tobacco habit.

We were in the midst of a trial in Court of Queen's Bench in Medicine Hat. The accused was facing a charge of trafficking cocaine.

Gwena Ozem, the Department of Justice Prosecutor, planned to call as a witness, the woman at whose house the accused was living at. There were some legal issues. He was married to another woman at the time. The accused was asserting spousal privilege which would make the conversations between him and his roommate, whom he was trying to classify as a common law wife, inadmissible.

I had mentioned to Gwena that during a smoke break, I told the accused we weren't buying it and that the police were investigating at that very moment his claim. His reaction and sudden change of attitude towards me was consistent with someone who was about to be caught in a lie. Apparently, there is legal precedence that allows testimony about an accused's demeanor and it all goes towards a reasonable assessment of credibility.

Now I'm not a lawyer. This was all legalese B.S. to me, but I had casually mentioned an insignificant event to the Prosecutor. Now I found myself once again in the Witness box.

The Prosecutor began by asking me, "Constable, do you partake in any particular vices?" Well, this was a cocaine trafficking trial and that question made the Judge and the Defence Counsel sit up and pay attention don'tcha know! Gwena continued, "In particular, do you smoke cigarettes?"

"Yes Ma'am."

"And with respect to this particular vice of yours, did you smoke a cigarette today during the last break?"

"Yes ma'am".

By now the Judge was scratching his head. Where was this going? Counsel for Defence just sat there, confused…I think his eyes were slightly crossed. The Prosecutor had me explain how during the previous few days of the trial I had taken the opportunity to have a smoke during every break. And during each smoke break, I had been joined by one other person, the accused.

I testified that he had been friendly and chatty during each of these "health club" meetings. Once the subject of the woman he claimed was his common-law wife was raised at trial, his demeanor changed, especially when I told him his claim was being investigated. He became quiet, nervous, and his hands shook so badly he dropped his cigarette. Apparently, this little bit of information was hugely significant. The motion to suppress the evidence of the "common-law" wife was denied.

I still don't understand it. Maybe I'll go out for a smoke and think about it.

The Czech Was in My Pocket

I can't remember the fellow's name but he was a photographer employed by a local newspaper. He was a friendly man and took every opportunity to chat up the Police, sometimes for his work, sometimes just to pass the time. He was a recent immigrant from Czechoslovakia and spoke English with an eastern European accent. He also smoked cigarettes. His favorite brand was those purchased by someone else.

I was at the scene of a motor vehicle accident and was currently engaged in the task of cervical immobilization. An occupant of one of the cars had injured her neck and as she sat in the front passenger seat I did as instructed by the paramedics and sat in the back seat, holding her neck perfectly straight and perfectly still with my hands until they could apply a cervical collar.

One of the paramedics scrambled to get the necessary gear as the photographer ambled up. He was very sensitive to the woman's predicament. He didn't stick a camera in her face and fire the flash. Instead, he asked me for a smoke.

"Uh Jeez…I'm kinda busy right now". He was insistent to the point where I finally told him to reach under my extended arms and into my shirt pocket, and to help himself to my cigarettes. He gingerly extracted my pack, selected a single smoke and lit it up. He exhaled a stream of smoke and muttered his thanks, leaving my pack on the car roof before he wandered off to take his photos from a respectful distance.

Fully Satisfied

So yes, I had a tobacco habit. Bare my throat to the world, I smoked cigarettes. And yes, I know that's not a healthy choice. And yes, I've endured many lectures by many persons, both known to me and from complete strangers. I have even been scolded by an obese person who was talking with their mouth full of a snack so heavily laden with Sodium you could have used it as a soil sterilant. So, pardon me, please.

I did try my best to be considerate to others. Back in the day when smoking was allowed in our police cars, any police car, I always chose to drive the oldest beast in the fleet. I didn't mind. While not shiny and new, all of our cars were well maintained mechanically.

To further keep people off my back, I made sure my car was always clean. Most guys would wash the outside of their car and maybe vacuum the floors. I scrubbed the black rubber floor mats with soapy water, cleaned the windows inside and out and washed down the dash and door panels. I had a can of aerosol "smoke eater" spray that professed to leave no trace of cigarette smell in the vehicle. The ashtray was always emptied and washed out before I left the car for the next shift. No one could say, "Eww...this car stinks!!"

Invariably, when I returned for duty twelve hours later, my car was a shithole. Mud on the floors, blood and puke in the back-seat prisoner compartment and the interior looked like someone had driven down a dusty gravel road at high speed with all the windows down. Drink containers and food wrappers littered the floor, left for me to clean up. I think it was done purposely, but in fun, because of the extra effort I put into cleaning that car.

One morning, I returned to find my car in such a state. As I cleaned up after the kid who drove it the night before, I found something that made me lose it. A half-eaten banana under the driver's front seat. It hadn't been tossed there absent mindedly but was intentionally placed where it was meant to not be discovered until it began to rot. I briefly toyed with the idea of wheeling one of the big, plastic garbage bins throughout the garage, making sure each car got a fair share, but abandoned that scheme in fear of staining the upholstery. So, rather than dirty the other cars, I decided to inconvenience the entire oncoming nightshift.

Some of our members were fairly large men. As they tried to get into their cars, they found the seats set in the fully forward position and the tilt steering wheels adjusted fully down. Once set back far enough to accommodate long legs, they discovered that the power seats had a vertical adjustment, and in the fully-up position, despite my average stature, even my head touched the roof. Past that hurdle? Well, the newer cars also had power adjustable foot pedals and in the fully-back position a twelve-year-old could probably have driven quite comfortably. Everything was wired to power up once the key was turned in the ignition. So, I made sure, when the key turned on...windshield wipers were fully on at high speed, the FM radio was set to full blast and of course, the siren, with a different tone selected for each vehicle.

It may not have encouraged cleanliness, but it sure made me feel better. And no one ever called me out for this bit of mischief.

Manufactured by Amazon.ca
Bolton, ON

12978798R00111